Endorsemei.

George Bloomer has a unique ability to communicate relevant truth in every language. This book, I believe, will bring revelation and answer some of the ageless questions that have been asked throughout the Body of Christ. I highly recommend this book to any minister, layman or member of the Body of Christ. This is a long awaited, life changing book.

Dr. Kingsley A. Fletcher, Senior Pastor
Miracle of Life Ministries International, Durham, NC

Witchcraft in the Pews is a most profound revelation of Satan's devices used within the church to entrap the people of God. This book dispels the darkness and brings forth the Light which enables the people of God to be loosed.

Rev. Otis Lockett, Sr., Pastor
Evangel Fellowship Church of God in Christ, Greensboro, NC

Witchcraft in the Pews was written to shed light on the fact that witchcraft is prevalent today, both within and outside of the church. Evangelist Bloomer's insight into the realm of the occult will be useful in helping Christians to gain a better understanding of how to effectively overcome the tactics of the enemy.

Bishop Alfred A. Owens, Jr., Pastor
Greater Mt. Calvary Holy Church, Washington, DC

Witchcraft in the Pews is one of the most powerful, informative, and truth-revealing books of our time. God has truly used Evangelist Bloomer mightily in this work. As an author, I appreciate good material. This is a major work making a great contribution to the Body of Christ.

Dr. Frank Summerfield
President of Summerfield Ministries International
Pastor of Word of God Fellowship, Raleigh, NC

In a day of compromise, apathy, and complacency, Evangelist George Bloomer brings a breath of fresh air back into the American pulpit. His unique ministry style of hard hitting Gospel preaching combined with his keen sense of humor is stirring up the anointing in the Body of Christ.

Rev. Ron Watts, Pastor
Living Waters Christian Community, Durham, NC

Witchcraft in the Pews is a most compelling topic. The response was great when this message was preached at Praise Power Conference in 1995. It has been a blessing to the conference participants and thousands of others who have heard the cassettes or seen the videos. This topic is a must read for pastors and church leaders interested in Satan-proofing their churches and equipping their congregations for true spiritual warfare.

Bishop Thomas Weeks
President of Praise Power Conference
Pastor of Greater Bethel Apostolic Temple, Wilmington, DE

Witchcraft in the Pews

Who's Sitting Next to You?

George Bloomer

PUBLISHING

Witchcraft in the Pews

Who's Sitting Next to You?

Printed in the United States of America
ISBN 1-56229-120-3

Pneuma Life Publishing
4451 Parliament Place
Lanham, MD 20706
301-577-4052
301-577-4935 Fax

Internet: http://www.pneumalife.com

This book is available from the following distributors:

Appalachian	Riverside
Spring Arbor	Baker and Taylor
Ingram	Whitaker House

2 3 4 5 6 7 8 9 10 Printing/Year 04 03 02 01 00 99 98

Contents

Dedication
Acknowledgements
Foreword
Introduction

Chapter   **Page**

Dedication

This book is dedicated foremost and above all to our Heavenly Father and His Son, Jesus Christ. May Their blessings be upon every word that is read.

This book is also dedicated to my mother, Georgia Bloomer, who played an integral part in my being here.

Acknowledgments

A special acknowledgment to my loving wife, Jeannie, who has patiently endured my many travels while waiting home, and raising our two lovely daughters, Jessica and Jennifer.

To my dear friend, Evangelist Sylvester Williams, who has stuck by me through thick and thin. Without his knowledge and assistance I would not have been able to complete this book in a timely manner.

To Barbara Williams, for all the typing.

To Pastor James Walden, who encouraged me to write this book.

To the many other Christians who played a part in this book which include Ernestine Stewart, Shimar Keith, Loren Coleman, Lisa Fraser and the Fraser family, Christine Liddell, and Bishop Weeks.

Foreword

The Lord Jesus Christ has endowed Evangelist George Bloomer with insight into the spiritual realm. He has engaged in direct warfare with the forces of darkness on foreign fields where he has traveled to preach the Gospel. However, let us not be deceived. As Brother Bloomer so poignantly points out, witchcraft is practiced in the United States of America as well. Brother Bloomer has remained humble as he continues to shed light on this overlooked or ignorantly dismissed topic.

This book is very timely because many pastors, church leaders and laymen, not knowing the truth, have been deceived by the enemy. The truth is that there is witchcraft in the pews.

Witchcraft is a true threat to the Church of God. Only by accepting Jesus Christ, the Son of God, as our Lord and Savior and knowing the truth, as given in the Bible, can we confront such error. This book is a must reading if you want to be made aware of the devices that Satan uses to confuse and divide the Body of Christ.

Dr. Ernestine Reems, Pastor
Center of Hope Community Church
Oakland, California

Introduction

In the twentieth century, witchcraft affects American society and many of its institutions, including the Church. This book reveals deceptions that many of us have accepted without question.

Have you ever attended a church where the pastor was domineering? Did he use fear to manipulate the members? Perhaps a faction in the church seemed excessively controlling and wanted to influence every decision. Whether these people knew it or not, they may have been practicing witchcraft.

Did you join in or watch the historic Million Man March on Washington, D. C.? Was this event a call to unity among the black race, or did Louis Farrakhan have another agenda? Through his speeches, Farrakhan drove a wedge between black men and Christianity. He introduced his audience to Islam, a religion that opposes what Christ taught.

Many churches have begun to sanction homosexual marriages. How has this deception crept into mainline denominations and Bible-believing churches? Satan uses sexual perversion in conjunction with witchcraft.

Do you consider yourself a member of the Religious Right? Do their policies coincide with this nation's Judeo-Christian beliefs? Were our founding documents written in a Christian culture? What should guide us in determining our nation's future?

The Bible says, "My people are destroyed for lack of knowledge" (Hosea 4:6). This book will equip men and women of God with knowledge to effectively wage spiritual warfare against the enemy.

Chapter One

What is Witchcraft?

Witchcraft is the art of getting one's will turned to yours. The Bible gives us three words that describe the occult: witchcraft, divination, and sorcery. These are the pillars of demonology. Let's look at these three words closely.

Divination is the fortune telling realm of the spirit. It works through tarot cards, tea leaves, crystal balls, horoscopes, and palm reading. Sorcery, which comes from the word pharmakeia (from which we derive pharmacy), works through drugs, alcohol, suggestive dancing, charms, and the ancient wearing of makeup. Witchcraft is the dominating realm of the spirit. It works primarily through disobedience, which opens the door for intimidation, manipulation, and domination. This is why witchcraft is alive and at work not only in our pulpits but also in our pews. Far more witchcraft operates in our churches than many of us are willing to admit.

Controlled by Fear

Raised as a Seventh Day Adventist, I encountered many new worship experiences when I converted to Pentecostalism through my born-again confession. Not spiritual enough to know what to call it, I sensed that my minister was very controlling. Later on I discovered this man even arranged and dissolved marriages.

Our pastor led a very dogmatic, legalistic church. His preaching focused on what we couldn't do. We were not allowed to play sports like other young men; neither were we allowed to date. During the summer we did not go to the beach, nor were we allowed to participate in outings that public schools. Everything to him was satanic. Later I realized that he was satanic.

After worshipping there for two years, I saw that the worst type of witchcraft was in operation at this church. This same minister preached at every service. We never held any revivals; we never discussed opposing opinions of theology; we heard no other messages from outside preachers. Our entire spiritual diet consisted of things this minister wanted us to hear and know. Each Sunday his message primarily dealt with hell-fire and brimstone. By instilling fear in our hearts, he controlled us.

What prompted me to leave this church? One day he told a story about a group of church people holding a conversation about him in their home. Although he was not present at this gathering, he said that the Lord allowed him to sit in on private meetings of members of the church "in the spirit". He claimed to know what everyone in the church was doing and discussing related to him and the church. On several occasions he hit the nail on the head, striking great fear in our hearts.

I often wondered why God would reveal my personal thoughts, prayers, and conversations to this man. I realized that I feared him more than I feared God. When I fell short and sinned, my prayer was not "Lord, forgive me" but "Lord, don't let my pastor find out."

How many churchgoing people today are presently under that type of witchcraft? Shortly after his death, God took me through a season of purging. The Holy Spirit gave me three dreams. In one dream this minister was alive. I had been invited to preach at the church. When he stepped on the platform, however, all the lights went out. When he had finished preaching and stepped off the platform, the lights came on.

God revealed to me that the church was in darkness. He had called me to enlighten His people regarding the awful, dreadful myths about witchcraft. There is nothing good about it.

How do so many people stay in these controlling, manipulating churches? A blinding spirit prevents them from seeing the truth of God, and many of them accept the lie.

Many preachers today are nothing but witches and warlocks in their practices. They manipulate the people of God and make merchants of them. They rape them of their finances and resources. They control by fear and false prophecies. Many of God's people have not been exposed to true freedom in Christ. Unfortunately, many came out of the world of sin right into the bondage of this so-called Christianity.

Satan uses ministers as his taskmasters. He has armed them with whips, formed from twisted interpretations of Scripture, to control the people of God. This results in deception, immorality, and perversion.

One young girl shared with her pastor how she had been abused by her uncles and a brother. She went to her pastor for help. How did he counsel her? He had sex with her for six months. She lost her mind and is now in a mental institution.

I am not on a witch hunt, but I do want to expose the devil and his deceptions. One problem facing the Church today is that many Christians have not been exposed to real Christianity. Many of us in the Church have come in based on our culture, religious affiliation, or church background but have not been introduced to Jesus.

What a frightening thought to know that many of us who repented ten years ago are just now finding a relationship with Jesus Christ. We have been exposed to doctrine and church order but not to the man Christ Jesus.

Can You See Jesus?

The prophet Isaiah said:

In the year that King Uzziah died I saw also the Lord sitting upon a throne, high and lifted up, and his train filled the temple (Isaiah 6:1).

Some people prevent us from seeing the Lord.

The Bible describes an incident where so many people had gathered that not everyone could see Jesus.

And again he entered into Capernaum after some days; and it was noised that he was in the house. And straightway many were gathered together, insomuch that there was no room to receive them, no, not so much as about the door: and he preached the word unto them.

And they come unto him, bringing one sick of the palsy, which was borne of four. And when they could not come nigh unto him for the press, they uncovered the roof where he was: and when they had broken it up, they let down the bed wherein the sick of the palsy lay.

When Jesus saw their faith he said.... Arise, and take up thy bed, and go thy way into thine house. And immediately he arose, took up the bed, and went forth before them all; insomuch that they were all amazed, and glorified God, saying, We never saw it on this fashion (Mark 2:1-5,11,12).

These men carried their sick friend to the roof because the people were too selfish to move out of the doorway. He could not get to Jesus because some individuals stood in the way.

The first thing they did was uncover the roof. That is what this book is doing–uncovering the powers of darkness. After they broke it up, they lowered the sick man to Jesus. After uncovering the deceptions of Satan, we must break up his strongholds and let the hurting, sick, and wounded come to Jesus.

In the same way that Jesus taught the crowd, we need teaching to expose the forces of evil. The Bible says:

Study to shew thyself approved unto God, a workman that needeth not to be ashamed, rightly dividing the word of truth (2 Timothy 2:15).

Satan wants to deceive us. He will even use an evangelist to attract crowds and attempt to draw people into devil worship. How do I know this? I experienced it myself.

Madness at Midnight

As a missionary, I was excited to be in the evangelistic field. Finally, I had a chance to share the gospel, cast out devils, and proclaim the acceptable year of the Lord.

15

My missionary journey took me to the bush of Jamaica, West Indies. I was invited to speak at a church that held 200 people. On this night, however, the crowd swelled to overflow capacity. Seeing over 500 people in attendance, I grew excited at the opportunity to minister to such a throng.

I did find one thing unusual, however. This church had scheduled me to speak at midnight. The darkness was even more intense because this church, which was located in the bush, had no electricity. They used candles to light the building.

As I sat in the pulpit, it appeared that we would later celebrate the Lord's supper. The communion table was draped in white linen with black tassels and white lace hanging from it. Coconuts, bananas, star apples, jack fruit, and a bottle of water sat on the communion table. Two women stood at the door attired in white dresses. They had red ribbons as a sachet around their waist and blue and red ribbons on both legs.

This did not seem unusual to me because we were in a different culture. Besides, I had seen much stranger dress in some churches in the United States.

The service proceeded without incident. Suddenly, I heard a loud scream that sent chills up my spine. Instead of decreasing, it increased in volume. This screaming only provoked others to join in.

My experience as a young evangelist had not prepared me for what was about to occur. I knew that only God could deliver me from this place.

One of the men sharing the pulpit with me, whom I did not know, stood up to say that I would speak after the *raising of the dead service.* My Holy Ghost boldness drained from me. Lazarus had already been raised by Jesus Christ, and I did not know of any other candidates.

This church also had drums. After the announcement the two women at the door drew out machetes and began to jump to the beat of the drummers. Two men came and turned the communion table upside down. They put boiled rice on this upside down table. By now the whole congregation had joined in with screaming and hollering. The coconut that had been sitting on the table popped open by itself.

I frantically asked God to deliver me out of this place. It seemed the situation only got worse.

The men beat the drums so violently that another man went into a convulsion and frothed at the mouth with every beat. That's when I realized witchcraft was in the pews. While everyone focused on the action on the floor, I ran out of the church as quickly as I could.

Later I discovered that I was used as a drawing card for this witchcraft service. Whenever an American evangelist preaches in Jamaica, he always attracts a lot of people. Even though they were doing it in ignorance, these people were practicing a form of witchcraft. They did not know that witchcraft and Christianity were opposed to each other. This experience, however, gave me great insight into witchcraft in the churches.

Opening the Door to Evil

Today Catholicism is the predominant religion in Latin America. Many of these countries practiced forms of witchcraft before the Catholics came. The military might of the European powers enabled their explorers to subdue these Latin American countries. Then the conquering Europeans converted the natives to Christianity. Christianity, as practiced by the Catholics, contains a lot of symbolism and rituals. These practices obscure the written Word of God and serve as a catalyst for their followers to drift into heresy.

Santeria is an example of heresy resulting from the fusion of Christianity and paganism. This cult is devoted to certain African divinities formerly identified with Catholic saints. Even though they may say the name Saint Peter, they really refer to one of their African deities.

Worship not devoted to God's Word will lead to heresy. The apostle Paul wrote:

> All scripture is given by inspiration of God, and is profitable for doctrine, for reproof, for correction, for instruction in righteousness (2 Timothy 3:16).

The Catholics tried to replace the Word of God with rituals and symbolism. This attempt has failed miserably in Latin American countries. The only way witchcraft and other heresies can be expunged from the church is by returning to the sound teachings of the Word of God.

We must not live under the mistaken impression that witchcraft is practiced only in Latin America. These practices are just as real in the United States. Just like it is disguised in the Santeria cult, witchcraft is also disguised in our churches today. In fact, I believe that witchcraft is practiced more in the churches of the United States than in churches anywhere else.

Infiltrating the Church

One church that scheduled me to preach a revival had been through nine pastors in five years. Five women controlled this church based on their ownership of the land on which the church was built. For two days I preached on spiritual warfare. On the fourth night of the revival, the five women came to church dressed in black. They walked around the walls of the church with the congregation jumping and screaming all over the place.

The following night the pastor told me to shut down the revival. The five women demanded that I close the meetings, and they relayed their sentiments through the pastor. Deciding not to leave the city, I continued the revival in a nearby motel. A tremendous outpouring of God's Holy Spirit put the seal of approval on the revival that had begun in the church.

An unusual incident let me know the message of spiritual warfare stirred the evil spirits in the area. One night I fell asleep in my clothes because the revival had exhausted me. I dreamed that little gremlins undressed me. When I woke up, I was wearing only my undergarments and a tie around my neck.

Another incident dramatically portrays the invasion of false worship within the church. After preaching the Word of God at a revival in New York City, I proceeded to minister to the needs of the people. One man for whom I prayed did not respond to the deliverance message I spoke to him. Instead he reached out, grabbed me by the neck, and began choking me. One of the sisters in the church cried out, "It's a demon!"

The whole church immediately moved to one side. I pleaded the blood of Jesus over the man, but it seemed not to avail. His hold on my throat only tightened. The old George Bloomer who grew up in the Red Hook projects in New York City showed up. I raised both my hands, put them on his neck, and began to choke him. I didn't let up until he loosened his grip on my neck. Once he returned to his senses, I cast the spirit out of this man in the name of Jesus Christ.

This man is now a devoted servant of Jesus Christ our Lord and works faithfully in the church.

Healed of Oppression

Young Witnesses For Christ Ministries takes me all over the world. We try to minister to the whole man–spirit, soul, and body. This occasionally means bringing food, basic toilet needs, and medical supplies.

I preached in the National Sports Arena in Guyana. Blackouts occur frequently in this country. As I was praying for people, the lights went out. Casting out evil spirits by candlelight in the name of Christ Jesus, I heard howling and screaming all around me.

A young girl with a disfigured face came to me. She had third degree burns over the corner of her mouth. She had confessed faith in Jesus Christ, and witch doctors had seared her mouth shut with hot irons to prevent her from witnessing.

Before coming to me, she went to various churches in the area to gain deliverance from the demonic oppression placed upon her by the witch doctors. The local pastors could console her, but they could not help her.

Because churches are not equipped to overcome the power of evil, many people seek deliverance but are unable to get it. Because the pastors could not help her, she went to the cults that communicated with familiar spirits. How did they try to drive out the evil spirits? They inflicted third degree burns over most of her body.

The Holy Spirit told me to stand her up. Once she stood up, I rebuked the spirit of perversion, witchcraft, doubt, and fear and ministered the healing power of Christ Jesus. This girl, who had been tormented and oppressed by the devil, began to renounce the hidden works of Satan. Her mouth, which had been seared shut at the corner, popped open. The lights came back on, and I ministered for another three hours. This scheduled one-week revival lasted an entire month.

How Does Satan Work?

To understand witchcraft we must understand the order of Satan's kingdom.

> Put on the whole armour of God, that ye may be able to stand against the wiles of the devil. For we wrestle not against flesh and blood, but against principalities, against powers, against the rulers of the darkness of this world, against spiritual wickedness in high places (Ephesians 6:11,12).

Satan's kingdom has four divisions. We find principalities or the domain of evil spirits. The word principalities is a combination of the words *princes in the palace*. In other words, evil spirits are territorial.

Daniel had prayed, fasted, and mourned before God for three full weeks. Had God turned a deaf ear to his cry? The angel Gabriel could not give Daniel the answer because he was held up by the spirit assigned to Persia. Michael the archangel came to Gabriel's assistance. When he finally broke through this spiritual opposition, Gabriel spoke these words to Daniel:

> Fear not, Daniel: for from the first day that thou didst set thine heart to understand, and to chasten thyself before thy God, thy words were heard, and I am come for thy words.

> But the prince of the kingdom of Persia withstood me one and twenty days: but, lo, Michael, one of the chief princes, came to help me; and I remained there with the kings of Persia (Daniel 10:12,13).

We also find demons, fallen angels, and seducing spirits. These evil spirits represent the power of the unseen evil kingdom.

The rulers of the darkness of this world refers to psychic hotlines, enchanters, witches, warlocks and monthly prognosticators.

Finally, we find spiritual wickedness in high places, preachers who preach against God in the name of God. This is where Satan's power rests in the church. Look at the false teaching that permeates the church, such as ordination of homosexuals, sanctioning of adultery, positive thinking, mental telepathy, prosperity, and "name it and claim it" theology. These teachings speak more to placating the desires of the flesh than to pleasing God.

This form of witchcraft in the U.S. is far more evil than that practiced by the witch doctors in Guyana. At least there the battle lines are clearly drawn. They know who the enemy is. The form of witchcraft being practiced in the United States is much more subtle and deceiving. Many believe they escape the grips of Satan when they join a church. They do not realize that condoning certain sexual behavior, teaching doctrines of devils, and holding services based on sensuality are witchcraft practices.

Origins of Witchcraft

The word witchcraft comes from an old English word *wiccecraft*. Witches use sorcery or magic to manipulate one's will. Witchcraft may be divided into two classes–natural and supernatural. One attributes its power to nature and the other to celestial powers. In practicing witchcraft man attempts to duplicate the wonderful acts of God either with natural products or the aid of devils. Sorcery, as generally rendered in the Bible, is the same word in the original text as witchcraft.

The word sorcery is from the Greek word *pharmakeia*. The word pharmacy comes from this word. Witches use drugs to deceive, seduce, and kill. We see an example of this in the Book of Acts.

> But there was a certain man, called Simon, which beforetime in the same city used sorcery, and bewitched the people of Samaria, giving out that he himself was some great one: To whom they all gave heed, from the least to the greatest, saying, This man is the great power of God. And to him they had regard, because that of long time he had bewitched them with sorceries (Acts 8:9-11).

How was Simon able to bewitch the people? He used drugs—pretty much the same way drugs bewitch us today.

The Devastation of Drugs

Young addicts never get a chance to experience the joys of life because of drugs. They leave their families for gangs. An ever-increasing threat to society, these gangs encourage crime and violent acts. In an effort to protect their "turf," gang members and innocent bystanders are often caught in the crossfire, resulting in needless deaths.

Much of the crime committed in the United States is drug related. The intense craving for their next fix has turned addicts against their own family members.

In one city in the South a young man so desperately wanted drugs that he broke into the home of his two elderly aunts and killed them to get money to buy drugs. Another woman gave her preteen daughter over to prostitution to supply her habit. Drug addiction affects the rich and poor alike. Well-known professional athletes lose millions of dollars because they cannot refrain from using drugs and get suspended.

How could drugs cause people to behave in such a way? Using sorcery, man tries to control with drugs and evil spirits what God controls supernaturally by His love.

Cocaine affects the same area of the brain where your pleasure center is located. This pleasure controls our sex drive and pain inflicted on the body. The body naturally produces a drug called dopamine that brings pleasure to the body during sexual intercourse. This natural, bodily-produced drug is released to mask the pain of injury. The drive to satisfy sexual desires within a drug-free person is just as strong as the drive within a cocaine addict to satisfy his craving.

Unable to break the control that sexual desires have over their lives, many people cope by getting married. There is not an easy way out for drug addicts, however. Enslaved by his addiction, a drug user must obey his craving whatever the cost. This shows the control that sorcerers have over people. They use drugs as a tool to get people to submit to them. In other words, your local drug dealer is a type of sorcerer.

God looked upon everything that He created and called it good. If that's true, how can drugs cause such devastation? The abuse of drugs brings about problems. Hospitals and doctors around the world use drugs just as powerful–even more powerful–than cocaine.

Why don't people get addicted every time they go to the hospital? Even though strong drugs are given to sick people, they don't get hooked because of the way God made the body. Whenever drugs are being used for severe trauma to the body, the body accepts the drug in much the same way ascorbic acid is added to juices to replenish vitamin C they may lack in the body.

Not all drug use is bad. When properly administered, drugs can bring about healing as God intended. When abused by drug addicts and sorcerers, however, drugs can bring about destruction.

Witchcraft is Supernatural

Some have the mistaken impression that witchcraft, the belief in magic and other diabolical acts, is mere superstition. Witchcraft is anything but harmless fun. It is about the control of your soul, mind, and body. Witchcraft has a supernatural element.

> And Moses and Aaron went in unto Pharaoh, and they did so as the Lord had commanded: and Aaron cast down his rod before Pharaoh, and before his servants, and it became a serpent. Then Pharaoh also called the wise men and the sorcerers: now the magicians of Egypt, they also did in like manner with their enchantments. For they cast down every man his rod, and they became serpents: but Aaron's rod swallowed up their rods (Exodus 7:10-12).

To show the power attributed to witchcraft and magic, the servants in Pharaoh's court duplicated Moses' feat of turning a rod into a serpent. How did God show that He is superior to evil power? Aaron's rod swallowed up the rods of the Egyptians.

Any supernatural power not of God is of the devil and is a form of witchcraft. We must be careful because the United States government has sanctioned witchcraft as a religion. Because they have the same rights as Christians, their influence can be very strong. One of the most celebrated days of the year is Halloween, the witches' Sabbath, when they gather together and pray to devils. The hillside strangler in California, who murdered a number of young people, was a devil worshiper.

Many countries openly practice forms of witchcraft. In Haiti voodoo is feared by the masses and practiced by the ruling elite. Cuba has Santeria, which is a mixture of Catholicism and voodoo. They may say they are praying to ancestors or inanimate objects, but in reality they are praying to devils. This opens up people to oppression, which may appear as mental illness.

Whenever someone appears to be psychotic, we often take them to doctors who prescribe drugs for him. Some people may have a chemical deficiency that causes them to behave irrationally. These people may need the drugs. Others are simply demon possessed and need to have the spirit cast out in the name of Jesus. One dramatic deliverance stands out in my mind.

Breaking the Curse

As we dismissed from church one Sunday, a young man approached me. He looked as if he hadn't slept in a few days. I also smelled alcohol on his breath and noticed his ragged clothes. Seeing a mild shaking in his body, I thought he might be having a nervous breakdown.

He told me that a few years before I had invited him to church. He decided to look me up because he was going through a difficult time in which he was losing control. His girlfriend had left him, and he did not know what to do because he really loved her. Voices urged him to commit suicide. The voices were so unrelenting that he thought about doing it just to get relief. He also revealed he was addicted to cocaine, alcohol, and cigarettes.

I immediately took him into the church and, with a few other members, began praying for his deliverance. First, I had him accept Jesus Christ as Lord and Savior of his life. Then we confessed the Word of God over him in prayer:

Greater is he that is in you, than he that is in the world (1 John 4:4)

For this purpose the Son of God was manifested, that he might destroy the works of the devil (1 John 3:8b).

We were not there long. When the young man stood up from prayer, he had stopped shaking. The drunken look had disappeared. He confessed that he was delivered.

This young brother often accompanied me to witness. His testimony stirred many hearts toward the Lord. One day we knocked on the door of a lady who was in graduate school to be a dietetic clinician. When the young man told how he had been delivered from cocaine, alcohol, and cigarettes, the lady stood in utter disbelief. She had learned that those three substances were the most addictive drugs known to mankind today. "Did you have any withdrawal symptoms?" she asked. Each drug by itself usually requires some withdrawal pain when kicking the habit.

"Never," he replied. Three months had passed since his salvation and deliverance. He had never experienced withdrawal symptoms. What an amazing act of God.

This happened because we believed the Word of God rather than the words of men. Jesus Christ said:

If the Son therefore shall make you free, ye shall be free indeed (John 8:32).

The world tells us that alcoholism is a disease and cocaine addiction is a sickness. If this is the case, we will never be free. God did not say this. Man said it, and we tend to believe man instead of God.

How can you break the curse of witchcraft? First, you must

accept Jesus Christ as Lord and Savior. You must also confess and acknowledge the Word of God in your life. God's promises can be trusted.

Your Legal Deliverance

What took place on Golgotha's hill is the basis for our salvation and deliverance. Jesus became a curse that we might be the recipient of the blessing. He was our sin substitute. Scripture says:

> And almost all things are by the law purged with blood; and without shedding of blood is no remission (Hebrews 9:22).

The blood of the risen Lamb of Calvary did not cover our sin but took our sins away.

We must understand that God is a legalist. He does not do anything illegal. The cross is the basis of our salvation. Faith appropriates what God has done for us. We must understand this as we pull down strongholds.

> For the weapons of our warfare are not carnal, but mighty through God to the pulling down of strong holds (2 Corinthians 10:4).

Satan is also a legalist. He goes by the book. Our adversary comes with legal papers concerning our bondage. The kingdom of heaven is likened to a courthouse where God is the Judge, Jesus is our defense attorney, Satan is the accuser of the brethren or the prosecuting attorney, the blood is the jury, the demons are Satan's police officers, and our case is before God in glory.

The Holy Spirit is the paralegal who prepares the case for litigation. What Satan accuses us of is true. We are guilty as charged. Because of the blood that has been applied to us, however, much of what Satan brings up is inadmissible as evidence. God no longer sees us in our sins. He sees us through the blood. The blood of a common man convicts, but the blood of Jesus acquits.

We must apply the blood of Jesus. What was done on the cross of Calvary defeats the works of the enemy. Satan is rendered powerless when we apply the blood. We can break free from his snares.

God promises healing and deliverance to His children, but that doesn't stop our adversary from attacking our lives. Satan skillfully misleads people and draws them into bondage. Many African Americans were deceived by a popular, historic, and seemingly good event. Let's examine the man and the message behind the Million Man March.

Chapter Two

Pharaoh's Con

The call had gone out. Old men, young men, and little boys gathered together. Professionals, common laborers, clergy, and gang members pooled their resources for a great moment in history. They came from the northern, southern, eastern, and western parts of the United States. Baptist, Methodist, Pentecostal, Catholic, and Muslims united for what some called a great spiritual awakening. Fathers proudly walked with their sons to form a sea of blackness never before witnessed. They gathered in Washington, D.C. for the Million Man March.

What caused this unprecedented outpouring of black brotherhood? What message did the marchers want to convey? Was their message black determination, political empowerment, moral rectitude, and the ability of the black man to economically sustain himself—or was it all a ruse meant to build the reputation of one man?

A Leadership Crisis

Many African-American leaders and organizations were opposed to the march. The problem was not the message but the messenger. The Honorable Minister Louis Farrakhan the head of the Black Muslim sect in the United States, proclaimed that God had inspired him to call for one million black men to march on Washington, D.C. His religious beliefs, anti-Semitic attitude, and racial separation views alienated many whom he was trying to attract.

Many within the African-American community strongly supported this adventure. These people were disaffected with the current leadership. Even though slavery ended in 1863, many still believed themselves to be in servitude to white men.

Anger and frustration based on racial discrimination, a conservative Congress postulated to be anti-black, and the continued lack of economic determination all bode in favor of support for the march. The belief that their leaders only pandered to the white majority served to magnify this perception. The time for turning the other cheek had ended. African Americans needed bold new leadership, and they believed this was the moment to make that statement.

This new leadership had to be visionary. It could not be someone with an old formula. The majority of the current leadership would not do because of ties to the 1960s Christian civil rights movement, which many believed had not gone far enough in bringing about equality in ethnic groups and economic classes. This indictment was not only against the civil rights movement but also Christianity, which was believed not militant enough to bring about the needed change.

Even though Christians such as Jesse Jackson, Al Sharpton, and Joseph Lowery are perceived as leaders, they were not seen as men with strong convictions. African Americans have a history of being very religious even to the point of suffering persecution for their faith. (During the civil rights movement, Christian ministers and churches persevered through the lynchings and police abuse spawned by racial hatred.) These men were seen as selling out their faith for the political arena. Their support for abortion and homosexuality, which the conservative black community saw as moral sins, showed betrayal of convictions.

The African-American community had sustained itself during the tumultuous 1900s by its unwavering faith in the Bible and gospel of Jesus Christ as the standards for all men to abide by. The black community believed that the clergy should be examples of righteousness and fortitude even if they themselves did not exhibit the same morality. Because there was no one else palatable to their taste for vision and morality, they endured the immoral message of leaders who were out of touch with their constituents.

Throughout history men with conviction have always received the support of the people. Whether right or wrong, those leaders who unflinchingly resolved to stay the course generated popular appeal. Consider the carnage that Hitler, Mussolini, the crusades, inquisitions, and holy wars have wrought on mankind. These episodes were precipitated by strong-willed men who stayed the course even though history proved their methods and ideas wrong.

Having learned from the past, today's leaders try to show their convictions in a contemporary medium. They know that, to a great extent, messages today are based on sound bites and photo opportunities–not deep themes. Most people are not economic pundits, history buffs, or religious experts who comprehend intricate concepts.

Because of lessons learned from history, many people are initially skeptical of leaders until the leaders prove they are truly concerned about their constituents. Therefore the populace makes up for this skepticism by looking to a leader who they think embodies their pain and disillusionment regardless of his true message.

Louis Farrakhan, head of the Black Muslims in the United States, initially appeared to be the reluctant leader. When the march was called–a march to support him and his racist views–many leaders cried foul. In order to mollify those opposed to his leading the march, he maintained that the march was not about him. In his opinion, it was a march about economic and political empowerment for the black man in America. He was only the messenger giving the call.

As it turned out, not only was the march a success (estimates range from 400,000 to 1,200,000 in attendance), but the one person given credit for the overwhelming turnout was Louis Farrakhan. He stated during his speech to the Million Man March attendants, "You cannot separate the message from the messenger," thereby implying that the success of the march was a result of his leadership.

Indeed, what is the message of Louis Farrakhan? Is he a modern day Moses leading the black people out of bondage in Egypt, or is he Pharaoh taking away their straw and telling them to continue to make bricks? Let's examine the Million Man March speech and the beliefs of Louis Farrakhan.

The Man and His Message

Farrakhan's speech revealed his use of numerology, an occult practice to discern future events.

This obelisk in front of us is representative of Egypt. In the 18th dynasty, a Pharaoh named Akhenaton was the first man of this history period to destroy the pantheon of many gods and bring the people to the worship of one god. And that one god was symbolized by a sun disk with nineteen rays coming out of that sun with hands holding the Egyptian Ankh–the cross of life. A-ton–the name for the one god in ancient Egypt. A-ton, the one god.

Nineteen rays. Look at your scripture. A woman, remember the nine, means somebody pregnant with an idea. But, in this case, it's a woman pregnant with a male child destined to rule the nations with a rod of iron. God is standing over her womb, and this child will be like the day sun, and he will say, "I am the light of the world."

Hands coming out of that sun, come unto me all ye that are heavy laden. I'm gonna give you rest, but I'm gonna give you life, because I am the resurrection and the life and if you believe in me, though you are dead, yet shall you live again. You're dead, black man. But if you believe in the god who created this sun of truth and of light with nineteen rays, meaning he's pregnant with God's spirit, God's life, God's wisdom.

Abraham Lincoln's statue, nineteen feet high, nineteen feet wide. Jefferson, nineteen feet high, sixteen [off-mike] and the third president, nineteen. Standing on the steps of the Capitol, in the light of the sun.

God wants us to seek Him for understanding and not meaning in cryptic numbers. How can anyone trust someone who bases his understanding of the plight of the black man on numerology, which is occultic? As Pharaoh trusted in a false religion in the days of Moses, so does Farrakhan. How could he stoop so low? Invoking the occult during such a great day for black men in American was a disgrace.

Indeed, the greatest disgrace was the number of Church leaders who were duped. They did not say a word against Farrakhan because they were more concerned about themselves instead of the sheep entrusted to their care. Not only is Farrakhan against the Christian faith, but he also betrayed the Muslim religion.

Farrakhan repeatedly made allusions to Jesus Christ as the risen Savior in his speech.

I love Jesus more than I love any of our servants. But I had a cross for him. I had nails for him. I had him to be rejected and despised. I had him falsely accused and brought before the courts of men. I had them spit on him. I had them to pierce his side. But, I loved him more than anybody else.

Why, God? Why did You do it? Why? He said, I did it that I might be glorified, because like Jew, no matter what I did to him, he never cursed Me, He never said My God ain't no good. He said whatever Your will is, that's what I want to do and that's why, even though he descended into hell, I have raised him to the limitless heights of heaven, because only those who know the depths of hell can appreciate the limitless heights of heaven.

Notice how he states there was a cross for Jesus. But he does not stop there. He also states that He was pierced in the side and descended into hell. Let us examine how this contradicts the Koran, the Muslim's book of faith.

And their saying: "We killed the Messiah, Jesus, the son of Mary, the Messenger of Allah." They did not kill him, nor did they crucify him but [they crucified] he [Judas] who was given the look [of Jesus]. Those who differ concerning him surely are in doubt regarding him, they have now knowledge of him, except the following of supposition, and they did not kill him—a certainty. Rather, Allah raised him up to Him. Allah is Mighty, the Wise (Koran, Chapter 4:158,159).

The Koran states that Jesus wasn't crucified; it was Judas who looked like Him. Farrakhan said Jesus had a cross, was pierced in the side, and descended into hell.

Why would he distort both the Christian and Muslim faiths? He did so because of his lack of integrity. How else could he be true to the mostly Christian Million Man Marchers and also be true to the Black Muslims? His interest was not in providing the truth, but only in honoring himself. Are we as African Americans willing to accept this affront to our faith all in the name of empowerment?

Black Muslims have their teachings based on the Koran, a collections of sayings attributed to the Prophet Mohammed approximately six centuries after the birth of our Lord and Savior Jesus Christ. Mohammed's teaching started Islam, and his followers are called Muslims.

Islam teaches that there is one God and that all must submit to His will. Muslims believe it is the will of God that the whole world be subjected to Islam. Furthermore, it teaches that the Prophet Mohammed is the chief and last prophet.

Indeed the doctrine that separates Christianity from any other religion, whether it be Islam or an animist religion, is the person and work of Jesus Christ.

And for their saying: "We killed the Messiah, Jesus, the son of Mary, the Messenger of Allah." They did not kill him, nor did they crucify him, but [they crucified] he [Judas] (Koran, Chapter 4:158).

Scripture contradicts the Koran:

Then released he Barabbas unto them: and when he had scourged Jesus, he delivered him to be crucified.... And the angel answered and said unto the women, Fear not ye: for I know that ye seek Jesus, which was crucified (Matthew 27:26; 28:5).

Our faith is based on the crucifixion, death, and resurrection of Jesus Christ. This fundamental difference puts the Muslim faith at error. For Christians to support someone who does not believe in the crucifixion of Christ is totally offensive.

Farrakhan and Muslims also believe that we are not to worship Jesus as the Son of God.

Verily, the Messiah, Jesus, son of Mary, was only a Messenger of Allah and a fulfillment of His word which He sent down to Mary, and a mercy from Him. So believe in Allah and His Messengers, and say not "They are three." Desist, it will be better for you. Verily, Allah is the only One God. Far is it from His Holiness that He should have a son (Koran, Chapter 4:172).

Jesus went up to Jerusalem to a feast of the Jews. During the feast, which occurred on a Sabbath day, Jesus met a man who had an infirmity for 38 years. Demonstrating compassion, Jesus healed the man. The Jews, however, rebuked Jesus for performing this work of power on the Sabbath.

Jesus claimed God was His Father. The Jews knew that this claim made Jesus equal with God. Jesus said:

That all men should honour the Son, even as they honour the Father. He that honoureth not the Son honoureth not the Father which hath sent him (John 5:23).

Jesus was emphatic. He ascribed to Himself the same honor that the Father received. If we reject the words of Jesus Christ, which were written before Muhammad was born or the Koran was written, we deny the foundation of our faith.

Even though Muslims selectively quote from the New Testament, they reject the gospel.

In the beginning was the Word, and the Word was with God and the Word was God.... And the Word was made flesh, and dwelt among us, (and we beheld his glory, the glory as of the only begotten of the Father,) full of grace and truth (John 1:1,14).

Jesus said:

> I came out from thee, and they have believed that thou didst send me.... That they all may be one; as thou, Father, art in me, and I in thee, that they also may be one in us: that the world may believe that thou hast sent me (John 17:8,21).

The apostle John and Jesus Himself clearly state the divinity of Jesus. John declares that Jesus was with the Father from the very beginning. The Word as translated in John 1:1 is the Greek word *logos* versus *lego* or *lallia,* which are other Greek words having to do with speech and languages. But *logos* refers to the mind and intellect of God. In other words, *logos* is the deliberate thoughts of God made flesh.

We can understand the *logos* and the mystery of the Godhead by using a cassette tape recorder as an example. After you record your voice, you can send the tape to someone in Swaziland who knows you and they will recognize the voice as being yours. You can be in one place and the tape in another place, leaving instructions or giving directions without compromising the credibility of the sender of the message.

In this analogy, Jesus was the cassette tape and the Father was the person speaking into the tape recorder. The casing for the cassette tape represents this fact

> God was manifest in the flesh (1 Timothy 3:16).

When Jesus said, "I and my Father are one" (John 10:30), he was referring to the inability to separate the recorded word from the person who spoke it.

> Then answered Jesus and said unto them, Verily, verily, I say unto you, The Son can do nothing of himself, but what he seeth the Father do: for what things soever he doeth, these

also doeth the Son likewise (John 5:19).

Even though they are one, they are still separate. The tape is in Swaziland, but you are in the United States. Just as the casing is inferior to a person, so is the flesh inferior to God. What is on the tape lets you know who it is. Likewise God the Father, being in Christ Jesus, lets us know Who He is.

Even though the Koran states that Jesus never said He was God or the Son of God, the Scriptures show otherwise.

Racism and Hypocrisy

Elijah Poole, who later changed his name to Elijah Muhammad, founded the Black Muslims in the United States. This sect started in 1934 during the Jim Crow era. Through espousing racist views, Elijah Muhammad believed that he could raise the black man's consciousness to the point where he could become independent from the white man whom he called the devil. To him all the world's evils could be traced to the white man. His way of eradicating the injustices of the past was to call for black people to separate themselves from white people.

Even though denominations, churches, and doctrines are sometimes built around separation of the races, this is not a view taught by the Word of God.

There is neither Jew nor Greek, there is neither bond nor free, there is neither male nor female: for ye are all one in Christ Jesus (Galatians 3:28).

And [God] hath made of one blood all nations of men for to dwell on all the face of the earth, and hath determined the times before appointed, and the bounds of their habitation (Acts 17:26).

Those who espouse racist views are not being led by God. It does not matter if they are white or black. If they practice such behavior, they are not led by God.

Louis Farrakhan has not repudiated the teachings of Prophet Mohammed or Elijah Muhammad; therefore Christians should reject him as a spiritual leader. But to show that he is an opportunist, Farrakhan went to the Sudan where they still enslave black Africans. He did not speak out against this inhumane treatment of our black African brothers. He betrayed the teaching of Farad Muhammad and Elijah Muhammad who were against the enslaving of Africans by going to a country that practices what his founder and mentor were totally against and what he is against in the United States.

How can he lead the black man out of his so-called bondage when he himself is a liar in bondage because of his rejection of Jesus Christ as Lord and Savior? Furthermore, Scripture states that anyone who believes that Christ is not come in the flesh is an antichrist.

Who is a liar but he that denieth that Jesus is the Christ? He is antichrist, that denieth the Father and the Son (1 John 2:22).

They be blind leaders of the blind. And if the blind lead the blind, both shall fall into the ditch (Matthew 15:14).

Louis Farrakhan, during his sixteen nation tour after the Million Man March, stopped in South Africa. There one of the directors of Islam, as was commonly reported in the worldwide press, said that "Christianity had failed the black man. The black man needs Louis Farrakhan to restore him." In one of the Arab countries Farrakhan was reported to have said that he wants to spread Islam throughout the west, especially in the United States.

A Return to Bondage?

How have so many Christians been deceived by this man who is trying to replace Christianity with Islam? Have the black men in America become so enraged at the perceived injustices that they are willing to turn their backs on the true God and follow a liar?

Persecution is nothing new to a believer in Jesus Christ. The Donatist, a Christian African group that arose in the fourth century A.D., survived until Prophet Mohammed came on the scene. They were willing to lose their lives at the hands of the Muslims rather than compromise their belief in the Lord Jesus Christ. We are not under the threat of losing our lives, but we are compromising the Christian faith by following an antichrist.

Pharaoh has arisen in the 1990s to recapture us and place us back into bondage. God told Israel:

Fear not to go down into Egypt; for I will there make of thee a great nation (Genesis 46:3).

God also said He would bring Israel up again. Egypt was never meant to be Israel's final destination. Some Israelites became comfortable in Egypt, however, and lost sight of God. Many started serving false gods.

The same thing is happening to African Americans. We have lost sight of the promises of God and have accepted a false god instead. We have embraced teachings and life-styles that are not godly. Instead of Pharaoh of Egypt, it is Farrakhan of Islam. Neither one could take the people of God out of bondage because they represent bondage.

Hosea says:

My people are destroyed for lack of knowledge (Hosea 4:6).

42

This ignorance creates a vacuum that can be filled with evil. No matter how well intended the leaders are, if they are willing to subjugate God's Word and proceed without repentance, the end result will always be destruction. God pronounces judgment on a people only when they refuse to repent and yield to His authority.

Who's Your Leader?

Today we have leaders who refuse to yield to God. As the Ford automobile commercial said, "Ford has a better idea." Many morally bankrupt leaders think they have a better idea. Like a reckless driver, they have passed all the warning signs. They do not realize they're hurtling over an open bridge. There are no warning signs or barriers to prevent them from going over the edge.

Look at the leaders who have been attracted to Louis Farrakhan. They're fallen heroes who are looking for a cause, any cause. Mayor Marion Barry of Washington, D.C. was caught on videotape smoking crack cocaine. Yet he has arisen once again to become a leader in our nation's capital. Ben Chavis, the former leader of the NAACP, was jettisoned for indiscretions related to money and sex. Now he is being touted as one of the principals behind what some say was the most successful march on Washington, D.C.

The Reverend Jesse Jackson, during his run for the presidency, endorsed the homosexual agenda and the abortion rights agenda. His liberal views have undermined his appeal to the masses as a leader. He is seen more as an antagonist to provoke discussion rather than one who can lead. Originally Jackson was opposed to the Million Man March. When he saw the groundswell of support for the event, however, he changed his mind and became a part of it. This action is characteristic of his opportunist style.

There is no need to mention that the well known African-American ministers called on to speak during this historic event did not once invoke the name of Jesus Christ. Jesus Christ said:

> Whosoever therefore shall be ashamed of me and of my words in this adulterous and sinful generation; of him also shall the Son of man be ashamed (Mark 8:38).

They prayed and spoke in the generic form of religion so as not to offend their Muslim brothers.

These are false prophets who have sold us on swelling words. Sails without wind and clouds without water, these men are intent on stealing our joy in Jesus Christ. Like the Muslims, they want to put Jesus on a level that denigrates His divinity. We must rise up and tell the king he has no clothes. We are not going to fall for the deceptions. Our allegiance is to the Father and His Son Jesus Christ.

It is time for us to turn to the true and living God and reject these leaders whose main concern is filthy lucre and media attention. God is the One Who sustains. He is the One Who gives us strength. Let us move on in the power of God and do great and wonderful exploits in the name of His Son Jesus Christ.

God has destined us to bring healing–not division–to the world. Why us? Because true love can only be shown by the persecution you are willing to endure from the one who hates you. Jesus Christ went to the cross as an innocent man so that the world may know the meaning of true love. If we really want to see God move, let us reject all hypocrisy and stand steadfastly on the Word of God no matter what persecution we may face.

Chapter Three

Prophet or Prognosticator?

One of the most widely-recognized scenes in Christendom today is believers witnessing the constant raging of spiritual warfare. Indeed, Christians are wrestling against those forces which are not flesh and blood but principalities, powers, the rulers of the darkness, and spiritual wickedness in high places. This is prominently taught, testified, preached, and carried out in churches and the actual lives of believers everywhere all around the world.

Glorified witchcraft is the terrorizing sign of the times. We're given the "signal" that this is so through the media where "harmless" spiritualists, palm readers, astrologers, psychics, witches, warlocks, wizards, mediums, and other types of necromancers, are having their demonic say. They speak and thereby curse the lives of millions of people. It's happening everywhere and to all kinds of people fascinated with, involved in, and advocating things of the occult and paranormal. It includes activity from the subtle forms of demonic in parapsychology, to the full-blown practice of Satanic witchcraft.

Interest and involvement in the things of the spirit realm–but not the Holy Spirit–is growing at alarming rates attracting everyone from the White House, to respected celebrities, to cultic and religious groups around the globe, government officials, high-ranking professionals, and the next-door neighbor. It is no surprise that psychic hotlines are a multi-million dollar industry, and that the ancient seer Nostradamus and his often timely predictions are experiencing a rapid re-birth in popularity. Considering what the Scriptures have prophesied concerning the antichrist and the end times, as we enter the new millenium, the belief will steadily grow that we are nearing the final stages of earthly existence. The adoption of false spiritualities, then, will inevitably prevail. But what is surprising, is that folks like you and me–Christians, believers, God's chosen people–have fallen prey to demonic practice and participation, as well!

That being the case, it becomes imperative to study these satanic spirits, powers, and forces leading the masses astray. The truth-telling is long overdue. The Bible tells us that the practices of necromancy and sorcery are abominable, and that the doers thereof will receive eternal damnation (Galatians 5:20-21). But those who believe in and receive the services of such ungodly spiritualists are displeasing to God and will in no wise enter into His kingdom.

Because of the spiritual urgency of this issue and the need for the proper identification and powerful eradication of these demonic forces we will investigate, define, expound upon, and use true testimony to illustrate the biblical, origins of foretelling, fortune telling, and prophetic utterance. We will compare these godly concepts to Satan's powerful but weaker imitation–seen in parapsychology practice–and consider how to distinguish between the two.

Prophecy

Prophecy, which the Apostle Paul described in the New Testament as a gift of the Holy Spirit to be desired and even coveted by the saints.

> But covet earnestly the best gifts: and ye show I unto you a more excellent way (1 Corinthians 12:31).

Prophecy is probably the forefather of what today is known as parapsychology. Parapsychology, the study of psychic phenomena, is a broad category where the perverted practice of witchcraft is taking place in the pews of our Christian churches and beyond. It is also how we generally define the spiritual initiatives of those practitioners under Satan's rule and stronghold. But first, a bit about prophecy.

"Prophecy", technically defined, is the declaring and predicting of future events, as influenced by divine guidance. Such spiritual foretelling extends from the anointed tongue of the prophet. The prophet, according to Bible tradition, was a man hand-picked by God to speak to the lives of God's chosen people. In many instances, individuals in biblical times who were not necessarily prophets by profession, would utter and give prophetic words and messages, as God randomly commanded them to do so. The words spoken by the prophet included those of salvation and damnation, of binding and deliverance, and were given expressly and exclusively to individuals of all walks of life. From kings to common men, countries and communities, or other associations of people.

The Biblical prophets of old were highly-revered men in their time, respected for their privileged communion with God and the sanctity of their spiritual profession, not to mention the accuracy of the words they spoke and events they foretold. Particularly in the Old Testament, incidents of prophetic utterance and biographies of the prophets themselves are most prevalent. We are told of the high regard given the prophetic gift in ancient times, the common fear, and the respect shown the prophet. The faithful people relied on the prophet's words. The relative fame of certain of prophets–Isaiah, Elijah, and Elisha–is retained even to this day. The prophet was God's messenger to the masses. He translated the blessing, or cursing words of God to His people and, on occasion, His enemies even when the unpopular sayings endangered the prophet himself bringing threats of persecution.

On the opposing end, Satan's twisted version of God's anointed foretellers is none other than the false prophet, or prognosticator, as wrong and rampant in Bible times as he is today. Several Bible stories give accounts of false prophets wielding their deadly, ungodly words, or practicing the sin of witchcraft. In 1 Kings 13, we read of the false prophet who lead the true prophet of God astray. Multiple New Testament tales tell of the disciples' dealings with spiritualists and necromancers.

Modern-day prognosticators practice in the same demonic vein as did those mediums of old. Astrologers, fortune tellers, palm readers, psychics, spiritualists, mediums, wizards, warlocks, witches, and mind controllers are in the business of rendering evil-based "prognosis", or foretelling. In all of the lives they touch, prognosticators wield an inadvertent curse. Even when the results of their prognosis's appear to be accurate and beneficial to those who employ them. The source of their prophetic gift is not godly. No authentic, long-lasting good can come of it. In fact, such people are deadly.

The power and spirit of the prognosticator is thoroughly satanic, as he offers his natural talent and gift to the prince of this world, to be used for worldly, perverted purpose and gain. Evil is the only possible outcome of that which these false prophets predict. I reiterate: Evil is the only possible outcome, result, and consequence, of that which the prognosticator predicts and foretells. This I know from personal experience. Allow me to share a little testimony.

Personal Experience

When the church I now pastor was in it's infancy, a most peculiar woman joined our membership. This woman was there even before the church was actually birthed. She became a regular at the powerful, revivalist, inner-city tent meetings we held in the southern city where the church now resides. These popular, highly anointed tent meetings were a prelude to the forming of the church that is there now.

Prior to the tent meetings that introduced this woman to our church, we saw several forewarnings of the satanic attacks to come upon us. For example, on the final evening of a three-day prayer meeting (in which individuals in agreement with the godly mission gathered and prayed on the tent site) a few of us talked and walked in the open five-acre field, surrounded by two housing projects.

Suddenly, a black van appeared on the street. Rap music blared as it drove around the field where we stood. Then, unexpectedly the music stopped, and out of the van's back doors jumped two young men, armed with shotguns. These men aimed and fired their weapons at another young man present on the same field. He ran in the other direction, but not before being shot in the heel. Just as quickly as it appeared the black van sped away. The young man who had been the target continued to run across the field, blood gushing from his badly-wounded foot. My partners and I turned to each other, and at the same time, spoke, "This is the place."

The following evening, the tent was erected, and revival began. While standing in a trailer at the front of the tent I spotted the peculiar woman. She sat in the audience wearing a straw hat and sandals, but most significantly, a tee-shirt that bore a written message. Looking back, those of us who saw the strange woman in the tent that night realized the prophetic poignancy of the saying on her shirt regarding her own life. It read: "Don't be hung by your tongue."

This woman turned out to an evil prognosticator. After that first service was over, she approached me at the front of the tent, and handed me a strange-looking piece of fruit. It was a red apple, with strange-colored streaks running through it. According to the woman, red was symbolic of perfection; green spots symbolized the young. Receiving the apple from the woman, I immediately disposed of it by flushing it down the commode.

Not long after she joined the church this woman would be revealed to be a manipulating, controlling, occult-dabbling witch, who had multiple hidden agendas and a cursing effect on the lives of the other parishioners. As it turns out, this woman was one who burned ceremonial candles, gave and performed satanic rituals for and against certain members, and tried to exact power and control in the actual running of the church.

On one occasion, she prayed for a certain young woman in the church, who, as a result, experienced nights of sleeplessness and stomach sickness. At another time, she gave a young lady in the church some articles of clothing to wear, but the girl never got to even try them on. Before this last incident with the garments, the Lord revealed to me exactly who this woman was, and where she was coming from. In the middle of the night, I was awakened by the Holy Spirit, Who spoke to me the truth of this woman's evil spirit and demonic involvement–that she was indeed a witch.

I forewarned the girl given the accursed clothing and warned her not to wear them. Not long thereafter, we asked this woman to leave the congregation by a general consensus of the people. Angrily, and after much ado, she eventually left. She took a few members with her who had fallen prey to her witching spell.

Nevertheless, if this woman and her crew had not left when they did, and taken their evil, satanic influences with them, there's no telling what undue damages might have been inflicted upon our newborn church, stunting the rapid growth that we have seen, with much amazement, thus far. Still, the Scripture tells us:

> All things work together for good to them that love God, to them that are the called according to his purpose (Romans 8:28).

I now know that our church's evil encounter with this woman was one that would produce a greater good: the Lord used her to initiate us into the fighting, confrontational realm of spiritual warfare.

Chapter Four

The Devil's Spawn

Demon possession has been a popular theme in the films of Hollywood and in science fiction literature. "The Exorcist," "The Omen," "Rosemary's Baby," the films of Steven Spielberg and the stories of Stephen King, all glorify the terrifying tales of the paranormal. Within the realms of popular media, however, the fascinating subjects of witchcraft, sorcery, magic, and the demonic, are often intended to induce fear or make a scary spectacle of glamorizing the devil. To most of the world, evil spirits and their missions are only the themes of mythology and imagination, and not reality. This is primarily because popular media, again, has not treated these as serious subjects and forces to be defensively explored and eradicated. Outside of the ranks of Christendom, and the actual, practicing circles of the occult, the satanic is all about show.

> For we wrestle not against flesh and blood, but against principalities, against powers, against the rulers of the darkness of this world, against spiritual wickedness in high places (Ephesians 6:12).

But the invisible "principalities," "powers," the "rulers of the darkness of this world," and the "spiritual wickedness in high places" are all very real and cruel. In fact, because these are not treated as powerful, menacing entities of evil, witchcraft, and all of its satanic variants exert the deadly influence with increasing popularity.

These foul forces are real. They are spirits that must be hosted by a living vessel to exact their evil. While demons have often physically been seen in their spirit forms by the naked eyes of man, it is most often through another man that we see the damage done by the devil's delegates. Not only is the soul of the possessed human cursed while the enemy lives within, but the lives of others that the possessed individual touches can be damaged or destroyed as well.

Satan's army is as nearly intact and skilled in the art of spiritual warfare as is God's. The devil has a million-man-march's worth of controlling commanders and manipulating men ready to attack not only the vulnerable men and women of the world, but the separated believers as well. Satan has an unnumbered host and hierarchy of strongmen attempting to destroy Christians' lives and revert them from the soul-covenant they've made with their God.

To each of the saints, there is assigned a personally-tailored demon sitting directly opposite the godly angel employed for each of our individual protection. These demons are professionally trained to strike us in our weakest areas, at our weakest moments. Only through the powers of prayer, fasting, and undying commitment to God are we able to shield ourselves from their daily attacks. However, when we are not spiritually strong and guarded, we become vulnerable to their satanic strategy and can be brought to our knees, or our graves, through a number of indecent, unclean involvements, activities and practices.

Perversion

Perversion is one of the primary elements employed by the devil to bring down God's people. Sexual perversion, in particular, is one of the most prevalent forms of the perversion spirit being practiced today. This is rarely acknowledged because of the shame and secrecy surrounding such abominable acts.

Nevertheless, this ungodliness is very much alive and well in the church. If we don't point it out and take indignant action to eliminate Christian's involvement in such deadly sexual persuasions, (pornography, sexual orgies, masturbation, intimate relations with demons, unnatural acts, and vile affections) then the Bride of Christ will remain defiled, impure, unprepared, and most tragically, unfit for the Groom and Heavenly Honeymoon.

Through counseling sessions, I've heard numerous accounts of demonic, satanic relationships with both men and women. The following is a story of one of the most extreme cases where sexual perversion lead to the birth of the unthinkable: a spawn, or child, of the devil himself.

Not very long ago, I was involved in a Christian tent crusade here in the U.S., where one night, a most powerful deliverance service took place. Over two thousand souls came to the altar, all being touched and released from whatever was binding them, by the shackle-breaking power of the Holy Spirit. Of these persons at the altar, there was one individual in particular who stood out. This attractive young woman appeared to have either a stomach tumor, or be several months pregnant. She approached the presiding ministers, myself included, and asked to be taken aside for a few moments, to share some things, and be directly ministered unto.

Once taken aside, this young woman began an open confession. She admitted to having been involved in indecent, sexual relations with demons. According to her, these unclean spirits would visit her in her bedroom at night, lay with her, and deposit their filthy residue into her spirit. She also admitted to involvement in the occult, though it had all started very innocently.

It began with her daily readings of inspirational messages, which she would depend on and take to heart, almost as if they were daily horoscope predictions, and evolved into her investigations into New Age-type literature and the consulting of mediums and witch doctors. Little did this woman know that one of the voodoo specialists she had hired to affect a curse on a lover, had turned on her and was now working for that same lover against this woman!

The information this young lady shared with us shocked and disturbed me. It caught some of us off guard. It seemed impossible that such damnable, foul activities as those described to us could be practiced by such an educated, articulate, beautiful young woman as the one who stood before us. This woman was not crazy, or feeble-minded. But just like God, Satan is no respecter of persons. What the young woman disclosed to us was all very true, despite her presentable, pleasant appearance, and the proof of her tale was soon to be manifested in the flesh.

Not long after the woman shared her story, she retired to the restroom in a building adjacent to our tent gathering, as she was feeling ill. By the accounts of those who accompanied her there, what happened next was very much like the scene of a typical labor and delivery process, during natural childbirth–almost. According to witnesses, this woman travailed in labor in the restroom, and eventually passed–the unimaginable–a ghastly, unspeakable, horrifying, nauseating, demon.

The woman birthed what appeared to be an egg. Not only was this exceptional, but this "egg" had what looked like a strange type of hair growing out of it, along with indented spaces in it's shell where two little eyes looked out. I saw this incredible, indescribable creature with my very own eyes, as it was brought to the sanctuary after the service. Needless to say, seeing this lifeless, hideous being lying motionless in a handkerchief was a most uncomfortable and sickening sight, one that would haunt me for many days to come. Those who witnessed it were completely outdone and even terrified. It was beyond gross. And yet, there was more of the disturbing and unexplained to come.

The still-born form that the lady had passed was soon taken back to the restroom, to be flushed down the commode. For not only was it dead, it was clearly demonic, and there was no purpose for saving it, or making a spectacle of it. It had to be annihilated, and the commode was the most convenient way to get it out of our presence. So into the toilet, it was dropped. Before it could be flushed, however, it sprung, suddenly, unexpectedly, to life, and began to move. Then, as if to beat us to the punch, it swam swiftly up the channel of the commode and vanished! Just like that, it was gone! Almost in the twinkling of an eye it disappeared with the express movement of a ghost that knows the lights are about to be turned on. Or, even better, the devil, when he realizes that truth is about to uncover him and call him by his foul name.

To this day, I don't know what became of the young woman who bred the devil's spawn. As the story goes, she had been placed under a reversed curse by a witch, by order of some man who had it in for her. Her own involvement in cultic rituals, and her tolerance and acquiescence to the demonic spirits that visited her in the night, led to her unnatural bearing. Her testimony, nevertheless, is a terrifying, haunting one, that should frighten us all out of curiosity, experimentation, and actual practice in the realm of the occult.

My personal motto is that whatever I didn't hear about Jesus doing, I don't do, and I recommend you likewise adopt this creed. Avoid unholy rituals of deliverance in the church, or visiting the local palm reader for a glimpse into the spirit realm, or chanting popular, "inspirational" sayings for daily encouragement. Don't allow the deadly, unclean spirit of perversion to lead you into sexual sin and addiction. When Christians meddle and play in the Prince of Darkness' territory, they become subject to his poison and laws of consequence.

Even so, we have the blessed assurance that those of us whose minds are stayed on our Redeemer:

Thou wilt keep him in perfect peace, whose mind is stayed on thee: because he trusteth in thee (Isaiah 26:3).

Likewise, the Scripture tells us that no weapon spiritual, physical, or otherwise—formed against the saints of God will prosper:

No weapon that is formed against thee shall prosper; and every tongue that shall rise against thee in judgment thou shalt condemn. This is the heritage of the servants of the Lord, and their righteousness is of me, saith the Lord (Isaiah 54:17).

Finally, my brethren, this story serves as a warning to those former believers in Christ who have now subscribed to the notions of Satan's sorcery, and have fallen prey to sexual perversion. For those who remain faithful, there is nothing to fear. For all facets of this accursed spirit of fear are completely cast out by the liberating power of Perfect Love.

Chapter Five

A Demon in My Bedroom

I'd like to share a true story that makes very clear the reality and prevalence of witchcraft in the pews of our Christian churches. It is the story of a demonic curse directly aimed at me with the most deadly and hostile of intents; a curse that could have prevailed in it's purpose to harm, or even kill me, had it not been for the protecting power of God on my side. The chilling effect of this incident has never left me, and every time I recall it, either mentally or verbally, I am reminded of how crafty and cruel Satan and his demonic commissioners really are.

Once while on the road preaching, I became reacquainted with a young lady whom I'd met previously. As we reintroduced ourselves, this young woman introduced me to another young woman standing there with her. I shook her hand and immediately sensed the foul nature of the woman's unclean spirit. As soon as I was able to I warned my friend her about her girlfriend. "Noooo," she laughed, totally disbelieving my words. "It can't be." I told her, in the most serious of tones, that her friend was involved in either one of two ungodly things: lesbianism or witchcraft. And possibly both.

As it happens, the young woman warned, eventually told her friend what I had revealed concerning her activities. This I know because of the demonic attack that soon came to exact certain revenge upon me. It happened a few days after I'd spoken the controversial words to my female acquaintance. I was staying at a local guest house–a private residence where I and a few other ministers on the circuit were residing. I believe because this particular house was within the devil's spiritual territory, what happened to me in the private room where I stayed was actually allowed to take place by the governing forces of Heaven. Ordinarily, such things would not have happened so easily to a child of God, but several cultic and satanic images and articles in this house allowed the evil spirits to enter my room and harass me there. For this reason I no longer stay at private homes when I travel. Of course, public lodging facilities have their histories, as well, so even when staying in a hotel, I take the time to pray throughout the room to dismiss any ungodly spirits and ghosts that may reside there.

On this particular night, I was suddenly awakened from a peaceful sleep, to what appeared to be a nightmarish vision: at the foot of the bed where I slept, there stood a ghastly, wrinkled old woman, dressed in filthy rags. Standing in a crouched position, she didn't look at me. She reached into a bag held in her gnarled hands and sprinkled a dust-like substance onto my feet. Horrified, I frantically pled the Blood of Jesus! It was then that a host of forceful, demonic black shadows suddenly appeared out of nowhere to grip and bind me in a powerful attempt to restrain my cries to God. Covering my eyes, mouth, and nose, these angry, unholy ghosts were cutting off my breath, draining the very life out of me as I struggled against their Herculean stronghold. In a fighting frenzy, I tried desperately with my natural, physical hands to loose their numerous unclean ones from my face; but they were spirit; and although I could very much feel them all over me, engulfing me, I could not easily loose them with my fists of fury. Thrashing my head from side to side to break free, I was able to loose my mouth for just a split second's time, long enough to blurt out a single word: "JESUS!" And immediately, the spirits fled.

Traumatized with terror, I jumped up from the bed and began to pace the floor of the room in frenzied confusion. Although my heart was pounding and I was sweating profusely, I still wasn't sure if I'd awakened from a nightmare, seen a terrifying vision, or if what had happened, had really happened. As I walked up and down the room, speaking in tongues and pleading the Blood of Jesus, I noticed an exceedingly foul smell had pervaded the room; it had come in immediately after the evil spirits' sudden departure.

Soon, there were was knocking at the door of my bedroom. The other guests in the house heard me loudly, frantically, calling upon the name of Jesus, and had come to see what all the commotion was about. Eager for the presence of some familiar, human company I allowed those at the door to come into the room.

As each of the individuals entered, they bore witness to the fact that what had happened in that room had not been a dream, nor a nightmare, nor a vision, but an actual reality of spiritual, demonic attack. As they walked into the room, each one asked, "What is that awful smell?" It was then I knew that the creepy old woman with the cursing dust, and the incredibly strong shadows that had attempted to strangle me, had not been mere figments of my imagination!

Later that night, I acquired the telephone number of the friend of my acquaintance: the vindictive young woman who had commissioned these evil entities of hell to come and destroy me because I had revealed her to be a demon-possessed soul. I dialed her home, and when she picked up I immediately told her I knew who she was and knew the evil she had just done. I proceeded to powerfully denounce the satanic spirit raging within and ruling her. She let out a piercingly high-pitched, angry, demonic scream. . .and hung up the phone.

I share this story, not to invoke fear but to illustrate the power and reality of Satan's demonic realm of evil spirits. Many Christians acknowledge the presence of the devil and his daily attack upon our lives, but we aren't aware of, nor fully believe in, the existence of Satan's hellish host of fallen angles, demons, and st013ngholding forces. It is most important that we know our adversaries in spiritual warfare. For if we don't recognize the enemy for who he really is, in all of his demonic variations, we cannot successfully fight him, or win the spiritual war.

Remember, "No weapon that is formed against thee shall prosper." (Isaiah 54:17) Christians are guaranteed victory over the forces of hell. On the night I was violently targeted by demonic spirits, even though the artillery of spiritual warfare was fired at me in full force, I still possessed the most powerful and lethal of ammunition–through the power of Jesus Christ, I overcame!

Chapter Six

Power is Nothing Without Control

I have concluded that we all want to love and be loved; know and be known; and, strangely enough, control and be controlled. Therein is the plot to the following story.

Some years ago I met a young man whom I will call John Doe. He was the friend of an acquaintance, whom I will call Minister Philip Gethsemane.

It was not uncommon for John's housemate, whom we will call Judas, to invite someone to stay with them who was a complete stranger to John. He may have heard Judas mention the person, but John had never formally met the man. Usually even the visit was a complete surprise.

John came home from work one night, greeted Judas and his family, the other guests, and then Philip. John sat down and joined the conversation. Judas formally introduced John to Elder Philip Gethsemane.

Philip said, "The Lord delivered me from a life of drugs and gang violence. God healed my body from all the trauma I put it through. My family wronged me and tried to destroy my ministry. But I didn't do to them what they did to me. I just left it in the hands of the Lord."

John was not a native of this city. His father pastored a church in another state. John had been sending his tithes home to his father to help support the ministry. Not only the son of a minister, John was also an aspiring minister himself.

Judas freely volunteered this information about John and Philip responded, "First of all, John, before you can pursue your calling into the ministry, you have to line yourself up with the Word. Scripture makes it clear that you are to give to the ministry that supports you spiritually. You have to be in the will of God before He can bless you."

That was John's first encounter with Philip. His story and reprimand were compelling. Having read John well, Philip had successfully gained the respect of an opportunity seeker.

Judas brought Philip to church and reintroduced him to his pastor, for they had formerly known each other. As was customary, she allowed the visiting minister to share a few words. Philip seized the opportunity to build his ministry in a new area, and in two minutes proceeded to tear the church up. But the pastor was more discerning than the congregation.

She told Judas, "If you love me as your pastor and if you believe that I am a woman of God, you will get that man out of your house."

Having been presented with such a compelling argument, Judas accepted her counsel and severed ties with Philip.

No Respect

By this time Philip and John had started to spend time together. John recalled a particular occasion when they were to meet at the mall. Two hours passed and Philip never called. John got angry when Philip failed to value his time–a sign of disrespect. Philip blew off the occasion, and John eventually calmed down.

When the two men were together, Philip proclaimed, "You know, John, I'm getting tired of you rising up on me. One of these days I am going to knock you back down."

Completely confused, John said, "Let me get this straight. What do you expect me to say when you rise up on me?"

Philip responded harshly, "Nothing! I expect you to take it. When I was a young minister, we could not even talk around elders."

And so the discussion ended.

Judas chose to keep his conversation with his pastor to himself. Heeding her warning, he continued to diminish his dealings with Philip. Thoroughly blind to the whole situation and not discerning the man's character, John only saw that Philip was stuck in a new city with no counsel. He rushed to be his advocate.

Judas had not verbalized it, but he did not plan to bring into reality any of the ideas that he and Philip had discussed before his arrival. John possessed many of the same skills as Judas, just to a lesser degree. Philip's first attempt to purchase a car failed so horribly that he was left with no money. His next project would not be so unsuccessful.

The Deception Begins

Seeing this minister's need to get established, as well as the personal benefits he could reap from the friendship, John helped Philip rent a house in the country. The bi-level home was filled with Aztec furniture. A glass sliding door led to the patio and backyard complete with green grass, rolling hills, clear blue skies, and even cows.

Next, John helped Philip to purchase a green, two-door Lexus and a fully loaded Honda Accord with a wooden dash, leather seats, sun and moon roof with a shield, tinted windows, spoiler, rims, and hold trim. Because Philip had no credit, John co-signed for his loan and he was approved. The final kiss of death was to provide Philip with a brand new Gold American Express card. John was tripping hard!

After Philip was settled, John decided to see less of him. John was beginning to think that perhaps he had made a mistake. He would make it to Philip's preaching engagements, talk to him on the phone about once a week, and see him outside of church about twice a month.

John got an unexpected phone call at work one day.

"Hello. Is this Mr. Doe?" asked the voice.

"Yes," said John.

"This is American Express."

"Yes, sir. What can I do for you?"

"Our records show that your account is past due."

"By how much?"

"The full amount of your balance is due. That's $3,500.00. Although there is an additional card holder on this account, the payments are your responsibility."

"I am well aware of that. I'll call you back."

John hung up the phone and called Philip right away.

"What's going on, sir?"

Philip replied in a monotone voice, "Nothing much."

"American Express just called me."

"I didn't get to send the payment in," Philip sighed in an embarrassed voice.

"I wish you would have told me sooner. When will you be able to send it in?"

"In two weeks."

"All right. I'll call them and let them know."

"Don't worry about it. I'll call them."

"The number is on the back of the card. Please call them A.S.A.P."

"All right."

John hung up the phone, but the conversation continued to play in his mind. He knew he had made a mistake. He bowed his head and prayed.

"Father, give me strength."

The Plot Unravels

Philip paid this bill on time, and everything seemed okay. The next month, however, he wasn't so conscientious. In fact, he skipped payments over the next three months and never called American Express. John called him faithfully every time the credit card company contacted him. During that time John began to get letters from the bank, and he called Philip.

How did this "minister" respond?

"I think they found out I knew Judas, and they just don't want me to have the car. John, I'm going through a very trying time and I need to know that you're with me."

"Of course I'm with you," John replied, feeling offended. "What does that have to do with anything?"

"Well, they're going to try to use you to get to me. Just don't tell them where I live."

"You don't have anything to worry about. If they take the car, that would show up as a repossession on my credit file. I'm trying to save it not lose it."

John was true to his word. He did not tell the bank where Philip lived.

Suddenly Philip stopped returning John's calls, stopped answering his phone, and discounted his paper. The reality of the situation hit John hard. He knew he was in trouble. Desperate, John did all that he possibly could to save himself. He and Judas went to Philip's job, repossessed the car, and took it home. John was devastated. He was $32,000 in debt, had two cars to maintain, and had a very angry American Express representative to deal with.

John finally got the courage to tell his friends what had happened. How did they respond to him?

"How could you be so stupid?"

"I can't believe you were so gullible."

"Were you sleeping with him?"

John was devastated. With friends like that, who needs the devil? It was no longer hard to understand how Job, a perfect and upright man, one who feared God and turned away from evil, cursed after only seven days with Eliphaz, Bildad, and Zophar.

Philip was one of the most controlling people I have ever met. But this story is not just about money. It is not even about Mr. John Doe and Minister Philip Gethsemane. It is about the rape, the physiological trauma, and the controlling spirit of witchcraft that conceives more rape, trauma, and control.

Who's in Control?

Unfortunately, mankind has wanted to be in control since the beginning of time. Instead of obeying God's only command, Adam and Eve chose to "be as gods, knowing good and evil" (Genesis 3:5). Even after God destroyed the earth by flood, the civilizations after Noah wanted to build a tower to the heavens.

And the whole earth was of one language, and of one speech.... And they said...let us build us a city and a tower, whose top may reach unto heaven; and let us make us a name, lets we be scattered abroad upon the face of the whole earth....

And the Lord said, Behold, the people is one, and they have all one language; and this they begin to do: and now nothing will be restrained from them, which they have imagined to do.... let us go down, and there confound their language, that they may not understand one another's speech (Genesis 11:1,4,6,7).

Men want to exercise control over the work of their hands, over their families, and over their futures. Because we don't have all the facts—or see life from God's perspective—our desire to control is often a curse.

But if we don't control things, who will? God has your life in the palm of His hand. If you'll only rely on Him, God will providentially guide you in every area of life. Trust Him to bless you as He sees fit.

What happens when men decide they won't allow God to reign over them?

> Then all the elders of Israel gathered themselves together, and came to Samuel unto Ramah, and said unto him, Behold, thou art old, and thy sons walk not in thy ways: now make us a king to judge us like all the nations....
>
> And the Lord said unto Samuel, Hearken unto the voice of the people in all that they say unto thee: for they have not rejected thee, but they have rejected me, that I should not reign over them.... Now therefore hearken unto their voice: howbeit yet protest solemnly unto them, and shew them the manner of the king that shall reign over them (1 Samuel 8:4,5,7,9).

God exercised control over the nation of Israel by raising up judges. The period of the judges began after the death of Joshua and continued until Samuel. The judges served a twofold purpose. First, God anointed the judges to provide deliverance to Israel from their oppressive enemies. Second, He appointed them to rule and administer government in the name of God. Scripture says:

> For the kingdom is the Lord's: and he is the governor among the nations (Psalm 22:28).

Israel accepted this form of control until the time of Samuel. Control can be good when properly administered as the judges did. It can also cause hardship for the recipients if not administered properly as some of their kings did.

Israel believed they could control their daily affairs better than God. They wanted a king like the other nations around them. They wanted to take control from the hands of God and place it in the hands of a king. They didn't understand that with control comes power. God's use of power was always just. The saying "Absolute power corrupts absolutely" certainly applies to man.

God warned the nation of Israel of the consequences awaiting them if they rejected Him, but they refused to heed what God spoke through the prophet. God never administers control without the consent of the person. If we want to throw off the yokes of ungodly control, we must be willing to acquire knowledge. Once we acquire knowledge of God's Word, we know the control is based on God's will.

Is Control Bad?

A little girl wanted to cross a very busy street to go to a candy store. Her parents refused to let her go because they knew the dangers awaiting their little girl. The parents exercised control for the good of the child. Moreover, this control is based on experience and knowledge of what could happen to their child if she crossed the street. Not all control is bad, but all control should be based on godly principles.

Control is usually set in place by a person or smaller group over a much larger group. Even though the black Africans outnumbered the white Africans in South Africa, they were still under the control of the apartheid government. As demonstrated here, control has nothing to do with numbers but influence.

Creating a Common Enemy

The person or group exerting control is usually very charismatic, thereby enhancing their ability to control. This charismatic person or group will usually create an enemy on which to focus the attention of the people or person. By getting you to focus on this adversary, you think less critically of the person exerting this influential control.

Creating an enemy also mobilizes the person or people around a common goal. As long as communism was perceived as a threat to the safety and security of the United States, there was little debate on the buildup of America's defense. Attention could be centered on this common enemy. When the major power brokers of communism dissolved, the perceived enemy was no longer there. Therefore people clamored to reduce the defense budget.

If the person exercising control points us to our real enemy, his actions are proper and right. If the desire is to turn brother against brother, race against race, denomination against denomination, or church against church, this control is evil.

> For we wrestle not against flesh and blood, but against principalities, against powers, against the rulers of the darkness of this world, against spiritual wickedness in high places (Ephesians 6:12).

Our struggle is with the spiritual realm. Those leaders wanting to exercise proper control must know how to address the spiritual problems facing all of us. If they allow the flesh to dictate this control, they are identical to Israel in seeking a king. They were ignorant to the benefits that result from serving a loving God and the destruction that can result from seeking another source of spiritual guidance. Saul, their first king, consulted a witch and died in battle the next day.

Like Israel, we refuse to acknowledge that God is in control. God cannot relinquish control because He is our creator. If we refuse to acknowledge God is in control, God will allow us to persist in our ignorance.

> Let every soul be subject unto the higher powers. For there is no power but of God: the powers that be are ordained of God (Romans 13:1).

Whenever leaders exercise control without acknowledging God, Who gives control, they are practicing a form of witchcraft. Witchcraft is the attempt to bend the will of someone to make it agree with the person practicing witchcraft. It is also the refusal to acknowledge God as being in control. This is why Samuel addressed Saul for disobeying God and said:

Rebellion is as the sin of witchcraft (1 Samuel 15:23).

Healing a Controlling Marriage

Control is demonstrated in many facets of our lives today. A wife may seek to control her husband by crying, threatening to leave the home, or using the children as pawns. She knows that she could never be more physical or vocal than her husband, so she seeks to exert control in ways in which she has power. She tries to manipulate her husband so that she has the advantage. A man may be unaware that he is being controlled in a subtle way. Moreover, if these attacks destroy the family unit, this control is wrong and needs to be addressed by the husband.

If the husband approaches his wife about misguided control without the right prescription for correction, he too could practice a form of control that could damage the relationship. The Bible says for men to "dwell with them [their wives] according to knowledge." (1 Peter 3:7) Before he can correct her, he should know why she goes to such extremes to manipulate the situation.

The man will often find a hurting woman who has become embittered because of her inability to express suppressed feelings. Once he determines the basis for her hurt, then he can more aptly apply the Word of God in a consoling, healing manner.

Sometimes a woman rejects the healing because the hurt may have been festering for years. Anything that took years to surface is not going to be easily soothed over. Therefore the husband should be patient when administering healing to a nonresponsive wife.

Hurt for the woman could have been at the hand of the man. If this is the case, he must first openly confess and apologize to the woman. Even though a man confesses his wrongdoing, it does not guarantee the woman will forgive him. He should not compound his error by getting upset with her for not telling him that she forgives him. Should forgiveness not be given initially by the woman, the man must be willing to prove he is truly repentant for any wrong he has done by patiently demonstrating good works toward her.

The woman, on the other hand, must admit that love and forgiveness are attributes every Christian should have. The same thing holds for the woman as for the man. If the woman feels she can maintain control by not forgiving and loving, she will not relinquish her control. To combat this, the man must state in no uncertain terms the boundaries in the relationship and what he will and will not accept.

The inability to forgive removes a person from the forgiveness of God. Forgiveness not only allows God's grace to be manifested in his or her life but also releases the woman to love. Many marriages have broken down because of the inability of one spouse to forgive. Jesus said if we do not forgive each other, our heavenly Father won't forgive us. Therefore, if we do not forgive, we are in danger of hell's fire.

A man tends to control by what comes natural to him—his physical strength and voice. Because a husband is the biggest and strongest in the family, he controls by physical and verbal abuse. The degree of force a man uses has a lot to do with what he believes he can get away with. This is why it is important for a woman to state in no uncertain terms that she will not tolerate abuse from her spouse. Men do not realize that such aggression is misplaced. God intended for men to provide and protect. Those big hands were never meant to punish the mother of his children but to hold and caress her.

A man without God in his life is a feminized man. A man can realize his true purpose only when he accepts Jesus Christ in his life. This is when he is truly a man.

The Assault Against Men

God has ordained that the man should be the head of his household. Why do men suffer more violence, a higher rate of prison incarceration, greater incidence of sickness, and a higher mortality rate than women? The devil is aggressively pursuing his goal to destroy the head. Men must accept Jesus Christ to thwart the plans of Satan.

In the old cowboy and Indian movies, whenever the Calvary was outnumbered, the commanding officer always had a quick solution to turn the battle in his favor. He ordered his men to shoot the chief. They believed that if they shot the leader, the other Indians would retreat.

Satan uses the same strategy against men today. His efforts have been somewhat successful in keeping men out of church. Recently a church wanted to add toilet facilities for men and women. The contractor said, "Based on my experience, more stalls will be needed for the women. Approximately 60 percent of the church population is female." In some churches the percentage is even higher. These numbers testify to the assault that Satan has made upon men.

If Satan destroys the man, he destroys the family. The decadence present in our society today can be attributed to the diminished role of the man. Statistic after statistic shows the greatest perpetrators of crime are young men who have no father in the home.

Society has taken away the control that God invested in man, declaring him to be "the head of the wife, even as Christ is the head of the church" (Ephesians 5:23). Man was meant to be the disciplinarian of the family.

He that spareth his rod hateth his son: but he that loveth him chasteneth him betimes (Proverbs 13:24).

Laws enacted to prevent child abuse, however, have handcuffed the God-given authority men have in the home. However, men do not have the right to brutalize their children.

Because of his physical strength, a family depended upon the man to plow the ground, sow the seed, and harvest the crop. Because of the remote location of the farms and the inadequate protection provided to city dwellers, a man often had to defend his family and land against robbers and wild animals. Today the local police serve as our protector.

The apostle Paul also spoke to the role of the man:

But if any provide not for his own, and specially for those of his own house, he hath denied the faith, and is worse than an infidel (1 Timothy 5:8).

The man should be the main provider for his family. Inasmuch as economics and skills determine a man's ability to provide for his family, they also determine his ability not to provide for his family.

If he is not able to provide, what happens? The government gives out food stamps, housing allowance, welfare checks, and medical assistance if needed. In other words, the government has become the provider.

I believe this is the reason so many women walk away from their marriages today. There is no drive to make the marriage work–or even get married–because of the illusion painted by the government.

Satan inspired this deceit, and many women have fallen for it. Just like the woman was deceived in the Garden of Eden, the same is happening today. The government has come in and enticed our women to have illegitimate children whom they cannot morally discipline.

God intended for a father and mother to raise children. Nowhere in the Bible does it say that a parent's ability to raise a child is based on income, intelligence, or social status. These qualities have been used as excuses for allowing or disallowing one or both parents the opportunity to raise their children.

The most important quality that parents should have is the ability to teach their children the Word of God. It is far more important for a child to know his Lord and Savior than to graduate from the finest school or wear the most expensive clothes.

Ephesians 6:4 tells us it is the father's responsibility to bring up his children "in the nurture and admonition of the Lord." Since Satan is opposed to the teaching of God's Word, he does not present this as a requirement to being a good father. Instead he wants to separate Church and State and eliminate the influence of Christianity in our nation. Satan, "the god of this world" (2 Corinthians 4:4), uses the government to set his agenda. He cannot control the gospel so he looks elsewhere.

Satan's Domain

What did Jesus say about serving two masters?

No man can serve two masters: for either he will hate the one, and love the other; or else he will hold to the one, and despise the other. Ye cannot serve God and mammon (Matthew 6:24).

Mammon is the riches of this world. Satan may control the things of this world, but he can't touch the things of God.

Just what does Satan control? Scripture shows what has come under his influence as a result of sin coming into the world.

And the devil, taking him up into an high mountain, shewed unto him all the kingdoms of the world in a moment of time. And the devil said unto him, All this power will I give thee, and the glory of them: for that is delivered unto me; and to whomsoever I will give it. If thou therefore wilt worship me, all shall be thine (Luke 4:5-7).

If we have not submitted our families, jobs, schools, and communities to God, they are controlled by Satan. The devil uses control in these areas to destroy his greatest threat–a born again man. Any man filled with the Holy Ghost and trusting Jesus Christ assumes his rightful position in God and makes the church stronger.

The devil is a lot like us. He only controls what he thinks he can get away with. Knowing he cannot control a Spirit-filled person, he seeks those that are not Spirit-filled. The Bible warns us:

Be sober, be vigilant; because your adversary the devil, as a roaring lion, walketh about, seeking whom he may devour (1 Peter 5:8).

78

Wherever he sees a weakness, he tries to exert influence for the purpose of exploiting that weakness for control. In seeking to please all religions at the expense of none, our government has shown its weakness to the devil. The devil has exploited this weakness, which we see manifested in some of the laws that have been enacted.

God seeks to exert control over His people. This control is not forced, however, but His servant freely chooses to be controlled by God. Any other control not based on the righteous Word of God is a form of witchcraft.

Chapter Seven

My Mother Is a Witch

In defining what witchcraft really is, we must look beyond the historically perceived green-faced woman with a black cat, riding a broom and cackling as she mixes evil potions. Today a more subtle witchery is taking place. Witchcraft and sorcery have evolved since Bible times, and now include present-day practitioners who study the ancient art and wield their wands in more modern yet equally menacing fashion.

For example, in innumerable cities, there exists schools, churches, clubs, and various other organizations, established for the preservation and progeny of the witching craft. Followers of "Hecate", the ancient, mythological mother of witches, are known by their dress, jewelry, and even now their license plate tags.

Cult religions, New Age followers, famous magicians, satanic worshippers, and practitioners of other paranormal and spiritualist arts, can likewise be classified as modern-day witches. All are extremely deadly. And yet, there is an even more subtle form of witchcraft being practiced in family settings and households everywhere–even in many Christian homes.

The witchcraft I speak of here is that of dominating, manipulating, parental control. Such is totally and absolutely ungodly.

> Therefore shall a man leave his father and his mother, and shall cleave unto his wife: and they shall be one flesh (Genesis 2:24).

The growth-stunting strongholds of mothers and fathers who refuse to let go, are wreaking havoc in the relationships and marriages of their grown children. Their over-involvement and desire to control cause many unions in Christendom today to fail. This form of witchcraft must stop! It is not the will of God that grown children be unduly influenced and persuaded by their parents. These parents must learn, however difficult the lesson, to cut the emotional umbilical cords connecting them to their sons and daughters, and allow them to properly reconnect these ties with their chosen spouses.

When a mother or father refuses to relinquish to their grown child to a daughter- or son-in-law, along with their child's future life and caretaking, it is often a direct carry-over from the dictatorship and spirit of domination that governed the household when that child was still young. Another common signs of control is favoritism to a specific child. This encourages unnatural relations between a child and parent. (2 Timothy 3:2-3)

When a mother or father esteems one of their children higher than the rest, it does not necessarily mean witchcraft is taking place, or that the parent will be a controlling force in the child's adult life. A parent's preference to one of his/her children usually means an indifference to or emotional neglect of the other offspring; quite often, this parent not only loves the favored child, but is indecently "in love" with that special little one. Such is vile affection, nevertheless, and the

Word of God clearly speaks against it. For not only can such inordinate love lead to further displays of unnatural affection, but it often has tragic, irreversible effects on both the favored child and the neglected one.

The affects of this unbalanced love is seen in drug addiction, emotional instability, psychological disorder, alienation, inferiority complexes, hostility, crime, extreme character flaws, and even seizures. Most often, however, it is the neglected offspring who reaps these problems because, his portion of his mother's nurture or the father's protection have been given away to the especially-loved child. In childhood, as he realizes his situation, he is too weak to fend for himself, or to take that which is rightfully his.

At the same time, the favored child becomes over fed, and tends to develop equally disturbing qualities, such as arrogance, vanity, weakness of character, over-confidence, brattiness, and dominance. All of these exaggerated qualities of the spoiled, specially-treated child are unclean spirits, which can only sicken the other members of the family, turning them against this particular child.

The parent who loves unequally, sows emotional ruin in the neglected child, and spiritual rottenness in the favored child. But God, Who is a just and fair God, can fully redeem the damaged souls of both of these children and will not hesitate to fairly judge and punish the unsuitable parent, as well.

The following is a testimony of one who witnessed firsthand the spiritual, emotional, and psychological damage by a parent's dominance and misdirected love:

My story begins at a time and place where I was not only beginning to know my new husband, but also became aware of a multitude of hidden, generational curses that existed in his family as well. Un-

fortunately, only after we had become a permanent couple was the entire truth revealed.

The fact of the matter was that his mother, my mother-in-law, was a witch. Not a witch who practiced sorcery, or who was into the occult, per-se, but one who practiced a form much more subtle, and less overt. Instead of creating magic potions and performing satanic rituals, her craft manifest itself in manipulation, domination, and control.

This woman had given birth to eight children. She had built a fiercely united army out of them, which no one could divide, infiltrate, or join without first getting the approval of the commanding officer– Mom. Even though she was married and her husband lived in the household, my husband's mother was the commanding officer in charge.

Throughout the lives of this woman's eight children, nearly every decision they made had to be geared toward pleasing their mother. They required her stamp of approval on their every action and deed. Not only did they need to be on Mom's good side, "or else," but her approval and acceptance guaranteed that the rest of the family would be in agreement. For any of these children, including my husband, to go against their mother's decisions or opinions, was to cut their own throats. The popular proverb, "Hell hath no fury like a woman scorned," rang all too true in this family which was often rigidly and selfishly governed by one.

On the outside, my mother-in-law was a normal mother–very caring, observant, nurturing, and gentle; so much so that I admit I respect her for rearing her children decently, and doing so almost single-handedly as their father was not actively involved. The children were church-goers–their father, an official in the church, and their mother also a church leader. But sadly the picture inside this unbalanced household was much different than the one presented in public.

As this mother ruled her family with an iron fist, the day inevitably came when I, her most recent daughter-in-law, was targeted for a

84

knock-out. *Her control and manipulation was so cunning it began to look as though I was the one at fault. To the family, I was the unwelcome intruder, there for the express purpose of taking her son (my husband), from his innocent, victimized mother. She claimed only to want to keep peace in the family. This entire episode came about when my husband decided he wanted to leave the family's church—her church—to join me at my place of worship. I had nothing at all to do with my husband's decision; it was a choice he made on his own. But, of course, this type of action went directly against one of the major, unspoken rules of the household: The family must stay together. In the mind of this dictating mother, if they did not all abide in the same house, the least they could do was attend the same church.*

So strong was this woman's domination and control in her offspring's lives, it spilled over into their marriages. Countless problems would surface in her children's marriages. But instead of these issues being handled and mended within the private confounds of their homes and relationships, they were either taken to my mother-in-law, or she would sift them out. Then, she would give orders on how to address the situations, instead of referring them to the Word of God.

For this cause shall a man leave his father and mother, and shall be joined unto his wife and they two shall be one flesh (Ephesians 5:31).

As a result of her inordinate involvement, many marriages were broken, and divorce and whoredom soon ran rampant.

I am convinced it was the spirit of Jezebel possessing this woman, and it grew with time, eventually gripping the souls of others in the family. In fact, the only difference between this woman and Jezebel is that Jezebel always sent a messenger to let her victims know that she was going to kill them; with my mother-in-law, there was no forewarning. The Scripture tells us that Jezebel had more influence than even her own husband, the king, who was known for his exceeding wickedness and control. (I Kings 21)

In a way, my husband's mother was even more dangerous because she used her wickedness and witchcraft in more cunning and subtle ways than Queen Jezebel. It surfaced anytime when she was challenged or confronted head-on, or when she went on a personal mission to exercise control in some facet of her family member's lives. And when her wickedness did surface, it did so through fits of rage which automatically thrust her and the person she was confronting into the realms of the demonic.

Needless to say, this mother's evil influence bred immeasurable instability, mental and emotional turmoil, and breakdowns in the lives of her offspring. These character flaws opened the door to drug and alcohol abuse among many of them. A spirit of favoritism also existed in the household. As a result, many of them went through their adult lives seeking approval from men and women in authority to feed the need for control established by their mother, and abate their feelings of inferiority.

These children learned to compete to win the love of both parents. During the holidays the race was on to see who could give Dad, and more important, Mom, the better gift to win the most parental brownie points. One Christmas holiday, I remember my heart broke as I watched one of the least favorite sons, proudly hand his mother his gift, while his father joked and mocked him in the background. His mother kindly thanked him for the gift, though it was obvious she couldn't have cared less. Throwing the gift on the bed, she rushed to open one of her daughter's gifts, as well as that of her oldest son, both of whom were the "prima donnas" of the family. Upon opening these two children's gifts, their mother screamed with excitement. The rest of the family rushed into the room and soon joined in her enthusiasm. Meanwhile, the unpopular son sat in the corner looking broken. He stared at his forsaken gift lying on the bed. The hurt in his eyes said, "Why did I even bother?"

Many of the male children in this family were filled with spirits of whoredom, yet at the same time, they were very passive. It wasn't unusual for several of them to form simultaneous relationships with the women inside and outside the church; and when they became bored with one, she was abandoned and immediately another was pursued. But their mother seemed to have no problem with this rampant promiscuity, mistreatment of females, and inconsistency in her sons. As long as her "boys" were happy and kept coming to church, nothing else mattered to her. But if one of the women involved with her sons challenged or crossed one of them, mother would step in and take control, always siding with her children in every instance, further encouraging their indecent behavior with her unconditional support.

While the males were very low-key and introverted, the female children were incredibly strong-willed women who stood their ground, even in instances where they knew they were wrong. Their motto seemed to be, "If Mom and Dad taught it, it is unquestionably right!" They refused to relent, even when the Word of God disputed their claims! These girls developed very masculine traits, and were always looking for a fight. They, too, experienced many broken relationships, but never seemed to learn from experience. They made it a sport to see who could belittle their man or their husband the most in front of the family. All of this unseemly display was about openly rebelling against the authority of their husbands and convincing themselves that they were in charge—just like their mother. This rebellion further proved the pervading spirit of witchcraft in the household—at first practiced by their mother, and then making bold manifestations through her daughters. As the Scripture tells us:

Rebellion is as the sin of witchcraft (1 Samuel 15:23).

Because this mother, was a crafty, subtle witch, she kept her in a protective, controlled box mentally, spiritually, and psychologically. They fed only on her narrow-minded wisdom. Her daughters were cold and selfish, her sons weak and unassertive. When the girls, in particular, didn't get their way, everyone around them paid the price. Giving and sharing failed to be planted in their spirits, even though they were faithful members of the church. When they saw others around them in trouble, they were unable to offer comfort or support. Instead, they gossiped and treated the person as an outcast, eventually driving them away.

The majority of these children went through life experiencing one traumatic experience after the other. As trial after painful trial came and shook their lives, they began to break from within becoming steadily loosened from their mother's vise-like grip. Inevitably, as they learned lessons the hard way, their independence grew. Their mother began to lose and feel out of control. Her children were getting involved in real marriages, moving away, and no longer consulting her for advice. God was beginning to heal them from years of witchcraft and bondage to this woman. Despite the sudden change, it was up to her to accept the move of nature and develop some peace of mind. If she had continued to try to hold on I believe she would have permanently driven away and lost her children, and possibly her own sanity as well.

Every way of a man is right in his own eyes: but the Lord pondereth the hearts (Psalm 21:2).

This woman, my mother-in-law, felt she had done the right thing for her children by dominating them and holding them so tightly. It is a blessed thing that God knows the hearts and true intents of men. He knew that this woman's misguided mothering was an attempt on her part to live out her dreams and aspirations through her children. Unfortunately, this is a mistake many parents make.

As Psalms 20:24 informs us, "Man's goings are of the Lord". If this is so, how is it that parents with a need to control, feel they must forcefully direct the ways and paths of their children even when the Bible tells them they don't even control their own comings and goings?

The story of my mother-in-law ends on a positive note. The bonds of control have begun to break and deliverance is now in order for both the children and their mother. Likewise, we all ought to revert from any and all spirits of control, domination, manipulation, and witchcraft that may rage within us and learn the more comely art of submission. In doing so, the lives of our children, as well as others, we try to control, will begin to heal. And at the same time, God will fill our own emotional and spiritual voids.

Chapter Eight

It's Happening
in the Church

A wedding is taking place in a traditional church nestled in the southern part of the United States, an area commonly called the Bible belt. The wedding ceremony has an ordained pastor, best man, ushers, seating for the bride, and seating for the groom. What's so unusual about this wedding? The bride is not female but male.

Yes, two males are being joined together in marriage. How could this happen in a Christian denomination that has long been noted for its stance against sexual perversion? How could it happen in a part of the country where the gospel is preached incessantly on television and radio? This is an area where Bible study is considered as important as the preached Word; Bible verses are memorized and quoted here as freely as a secular person would quote Shakespeare or sections of the United States Constitution.

What is taking place in the church is not unique. God has given us Scripture as an example so that we do not fall into the same condemnation of the disobedient men recorded in the Bible.

Now these things happened unto them for ensamples: and they are written for our admonition, upon whom the ends of the world are come (1 Corinthians 10:11).

Let's look at Israel in the Old Testament to better understand some of the ungodly things being foisted upon us.

False Worship

Because of Solomon's sins, God split the nation of Israel into two kingdoms after his death. The northern kingdom was called Israel and the southern kingdom Judah. Jeroboam, a servant of Solomon, was called by God to rule the northern kingdom. (See 1 King 11:29-40.) God told Jeroboam that He would bless Israel as long as the nation obeyed Him.

Jeroboam, however, fell into some of the same traps that church leaders are falling into today. The first northern kingdom leader was fearful of losing his kingdom to the southern kingdom of Judah.

The temple, the official place of worship, was located in the southern kingdom. Both the northern and southern kingdoms were to offer their sacrifices and attend designated feasts at the temple. Jeroboam feared that his people would desert the northern kingdom and settle in the southern kingdom because they frequently visited the south. His fear, however, had no substantiation. Instead of Jeroboam trusting God, he accepted the counsel of foolish men.

Whenever people do not obtain the holiness of God through Christ Jesus because of their love for the world, they often try to counterfeit what is good to make themselves appear good. The Bible says, "Satan himself is transformed into an angel of light" (2 Corinthians 11:14). Based on the foolish counsel of his men, Jeroboam set up counterfeit worship in the northern kingdom.

The Israelites set up two temples; one in the land of Dan and the other in Bethel. They appointed prophets and priests to minister in the temples. They also had their holy days set aside. What was missing? They had replaced Jehovah with false gods.

> But the hour cometh, and now is, when the true worshippers shall worship the Father in spirit and in truth: for the Father seeketh such to worship him. God is a Spirit: and they that worship him must worship him in spirit and in truth (John 4:23,24).

They were worshipping but not in spirit nor in truth. Because of this, God pronounced judgment on the northern kingdom. The Assyrians deported the northern kingdom from their land because of their sins. Jeroboam's name has since been spoken of derisively by the Jews as a result of the role he played in leading the northern kingdom astray.

Just as Jeroboam instituted false worship, so have many churches and church leaders. They have pastors, teachers, deacons, the Bible, and inspirational songs sung each Sunday. Externally, just as in the northern kingdom of Jeroboam, everything appears to be right. They are not worshipping God in spirit and in truth, however.

Misplaced love causes us to drift into false worship. The Church has lost its first love and replaced it with the love of the world.

> Love not the world, neither the things that are in the world. If any man love the world, the love of the Father is not in him. For all that is in the world, the lust of the flesh, and the lust of the eyes, and the pride of life, is not of the Father, but is of the world (1 John 2:15,16).

Why is the Church so easily seduced? We love the world more than we love God.

Defiled by Sexual Sin

Homosexuality is not the only sin that has taken root within the Church. God warned the Israelites that indulging in any type of sexual sin, like the heathen nations that surrounded them, would defile them.

> And the Lord spake unto Moses, saying, Speak unto the children of Israel, and say unto them, I am the Lord your God. After the doings of the land of Egypt, wherein ye dwelt, ye shall not do: and after the doings of the land of Canaan, whither I bring you, shall ye not do: neither shall ye walk in their ordinances....
>
> Defile not ye yourselves in any of these things: for in all these the nations are defiled which I cast out before you (Leviticus 18:1-3,24).

Leviticus 18 lists sexual sins expressly forbidden by God that pervade the Church today. This includes incest, adultery, bestiality, and homosexuality. Pagan nations served their idol gods by indulging in such deviant practices. The Lord graphically showed the condition of people who do not know Him. In other words, your sexual life-style determines your relationship to God.

Let us look at these sins more closely to see their relationship to witchcraft. The word homosexuality is not used in the Bible, but certain terms refer to this practice. Genesis 19 shows us the origin of the word sodomite and how its meaning was derived.

> But before they lay down, the men of the city, even the men of Sodom, compassed the house round, both old and young, all the people from every quarter: And they called unto Lot, and said unto him, Where are the men which came in to thee this night? bring them out unto us, that we may know them.

And Lot went out at the door unto them, and shut the door after him, and said, I pray you, brethren, do not so wickedly. Behold now, I have two daughters which have not known man; let me, I pray you, bring them out unto you, and do ye to them as is good in your eyes: only unto these men do nothing; for therefore came they under the shadow of my roof.

And they said, Stand back. And they said again, This one fellow came in to sojourn, and he will needs be a judge: now will we deal worse with thee, than with them. And they pressed sore upon the man, even Lot, and came near to break the door. But the men put forth their hand, and pulled Lot into the house to them, and shut to the door (Genesis 19:4-10).

This act was so reprehensible that God strictly forbade the admittance of a sodomite into the congregation of the Lord.

He that is wounded in the stones, or hath his privy member cut off, shall not enter into the congregation of the Lord....

There shall be no whore of the daughters of Israel, nor a sodomite of the sons of Israel. Thou shall not bring the hire of a whore, or the price of a dog, into the house of the Lord thy God for any vow: for even both these are abomination unto the Lord thy God (Deuteronomy 23:1,17,18).

The men of Sodom were seeking to have sexual intercourse with the angels of God. This is how the term sodomite came about. Men having sexual intercourse with another man. What does the New Testament have to say about these sexual practices?

Wherefore God also gave them up to uncleanness through the lusts of their own hearts, to dishonour their own bodies between themselves: Who changed the truth of God into a lie, and worshipped and served the creature more than the Creator....

For this cause God gave them up unto vile affections: for even their women did change the natural use into that which is against nature: And likewise also the men, leaving the natural use of the woman, burned in their lust one toward another; men with men working that which is unseemly, and receiving in themselves that recompense of their error which was meet.

And even as they did not like to retain God in their knowledge, God gave them over to a reprobate mind, to do those things which are not convenient (Romans 1:24,26-28).

He saith unto them, Moses because of the hardness of your hearts suffered you to put away your wives: but from the beginning it was not so (Matthew 19:8).

Jesus and the apostle Paul, the writer of Romans, states that we enter into homosexuality and adultery when we have turned from God. Many believe that sexual perverseness starts the downward spiral from God. Jesus and Paul, under the inspiration of the Holy Spirit, state a person in such a condition has already departed from God. Notice the words "did not like to retain God in their knowledge. . ." and "because of the hardness of your hearts." These are conditions of a person who has rejected God. Therefore God leaves him to his own devices.

Mystery of the Six Little Men

Without realizing it, many Christians possess and use articles of evil in all aspects of life including wearing historically satanic and cultic jewelry, bringing the "Christmas Spirit" boxes into their homes, displaying spiritually meaningful garments and artwork on bodies and in homes, and purchasing toys for their children (including some of the eerie, demonically suggestive action figurines, and dolls of African religion, ritual, and voodoo).

Believers unknowingly embrace the spirit of witchcraft. But they are not without exemption from the curses that these Satanic articles bring. The Bible says we are to bring no accursed thing into our homes.

And ye, in any wise keep yourselves from the accursed thing, lest ye make yourselves accursed, when ye take of the accursed thing, and make the camp of Israel a curse, and trouble(Joshua 6:18).

Many consider such everyday items as the ones described above to be harmless, and see them having nothing to do with witchcraft. But the spirits that have possessed these articles throughout history have never left them and are just as strong today. What's more, voodoo, witchcraft, and sorcery are very much alive and thriving. New curses are being exacted in peoples' lives by the practitioners of these ancient religions and cults.

What continues to surprise me is that we watch programs and hear about ancient curses on the thrones of King Tut and others. We visit these places, and yet bring articles representing these empires into our homes. We can never be too careful when bringing such souvenirs, symbolic stones, and other memorabilia, into our lives and the private spaces where we dwell. Once such items cross the thresholds of our homes, we inadvertently invite the devil in for a permanent visit.

One such family possessed a seemingly harmless souvenir. It turned out to contain a world of satanic meaning and influenced the lives of each member of the household for the worse.

It began as a Christmas gift presented to the young lady who told me the story, when she was in grade school. She kept the gift for thirteen years before handing it over to me.

Knowing my popular teachings on current-day witchcraft in the Christian church, this young lady thought some of the dolls in her home might actually be of voodoo, or satanic origin. Not long thereafter, she presented to me what looked like a little gift box. Light and small enough to fit in the palm of my hand, the little box was made of bamboo, with colorful markings made from berry dye. The bright-colored stripes on the box were painted in such a way as to make it look almost like a basket.

The box was very delicate, almost fragile in construction, and was covered by a lift-off lid. Upon opening it, one who was uninformed might have been delightfully surprised to see what lay inside: six tiny little human figures, constructed of a thin, brown fiber lay toppled upon one another. All of these little men had ink markings on their heads to illustrate eyes and hair and were colorfully dressed in strong weaving thread. Along with the little dolls, there was a tiny, printed note inside the box, which read:

> *The children of Guatemala are told that these dolls are available to hear and take care of their worries. Each night, before going to sleep, the children pray to the dolls with their concerns. But they can only have six worries each night.*

As I received the bamboo box from the girl, I shook the six tiny figures into my hand. No doubt about it, these were satanic, voodoo dolls. Not only was this obvious by simply looking at the dolls, but the note that accompanied them told the whole story of their spirit and purpose. Immediately, I questioned the young lady about where the dolls had come from, how long they had been in the home, and if she had ever consulted or prayed to them. She told me the box had been innocently given by a relative and they had been in the home for over a decade. On several occasions, she took the dolls out of the box, held them in her hands, and prayed to them.

I took immediate action to bind the curse that had undoubtedly been placed in her life by these demonic characters that now sat before me. I led this young lady in a prayer of repentance, and denounced satanic attack and influence. We broke the spiritual curse and wicked stronghold of the enemy in her life. She is now growing and walking in the knowledge of the truth.

In the meantime, I started researching into the history, meaning, power, and mystery of these six little men in a tiny box. It was no coincidence, I believe, that six little men resided in the box, because in the family of this girl there were six members of the household—a specific demon for each of them. According to a specialist on things of the occult, the spirits of the figures in such boxes control the inhabitants of the house where they dwelt, through their persons' dreams and imagination. If there weren't little men in the little bamboo boxes, symbolic animals, such as the bird, the cat, and the dog, were used. Each of these animal spirits had a specific mission and purpose to exact on an individual's life. According to a book of enchantments owned by this specialist, the bird spirit was represented by wind and was meant to induce a lifting. The cat spirit, on the other hand, brought trouble. Finally, the dog spirit brought protection to a person's life. According to the specialist, the spirits were awarded their power through the action of the individual who possessed them, the evil-doer who placed them there. When these little dolls were taken out of the box and held in hand, or even when the tops of the boxes that contained these figures were lifted off, their spirits were released into the house to work their demonic magic.

The young lady who showed me the strange box, believes the spirit of the six men affected the lives of her family members. Several unusual and unnatural events had occurred over the thirteen years in which she owned the box. The family had experienced the inability to stay in one place of residence, for more than a year at a time. During a nine year period of time the family lived in at least twelve residences. In addition to this lack of stability the family had also experienced stunting financial instability, never able to break free from the spirit of poverty. A final unusual happening was the unnatural swelling of each of the female members' left ankles, except for the youngest who just happened to have moved from the household.

It is not always easily determined where the evil influence in the life of an individual originates. But in the case of this young lady and her family, the mystery was revealed. The demonic presence of these accursed dolls–these "innocent", "harmless", "meaningless" figures–caused them so much turmoil. Nevertheless, through the demon-binding power of the Holy Spirit, the shackles of poverty, sickness, and instability that plagued them through years, are being slowly but surely irradicated.

How is This Related to Witchcraft?

Witchcraft is any religion that is not Christ-centered through obedience to His Word. Therefore all pagan religions are based in witchcraft. Even though the sign outside the building may say church, the practices within say paganism.

Who are the spiritual heads of the occult or pagan religions? The apostle Paul said that the heads are devils. People who indulge in sexual perversion practice witchcraft within the Church.

But I say, that the things which the Gentiles sacrifice, they sacrifice to devils, and not to God: and I would not that ye should have fellowship with devils (1 Corinthians. 10:20).

The Church, once considered the place to receive teachings on proper moral behavior and also see it practiced, is under attack. This attack is not from without but within. Clergy and lay members alike are being seduced by carnal pleasures.

> Now the Spirit speaketh expressly, that in the latter times some shall depart from the faith, giving heed to seducing spirits, and doctrines of devils (1 Timothy 4:1).

This seduction, as demonstrated by the homosexual wedding, has taken root within the Church. Not only do some pastors solemnize homosexual relationships, but they also condone them or blindly look the other way when they come into the Church. Our choirs, usher boards, trustee boards, and auxiliaries are being infiltrated by this debased life-style. How many effeminate gospel singers or musicians have you seen? Some are outright homosexuals. Churches tolerate this behavior for all the wrong reasons.

The Wrong Focus

Some ministers are people counters. They could not care less about the destiny of a person's soul as long as others perceive their church as successful based on the number of people sitting in their pews. Jesus declared:

> No man cometh unto the Father, but by me" (John 14:6).

Because He stood resolutely on His ministry and did not waver, many disciples ceased to walk with Him. Jesus even turned to the twelve disciples and asked:

> Will ye also go away? (John 6:67).

Jesus loved everyone. He showed His disciples that it was not the great crowds following Him that constituted righteousness but those willing to do the will of His Father—even if it meant no one following Him. Jesus demonstrated that quality is more important than quantity.

Other ministers have fallen into this trap: They cannot financially support the kingdom of God without using depraved sinners as a drawing card to raise funds. They sponsor concerts and fund-raisers that focus on giving more glory to men than to God. They forget the words of the apostle Paul:

> My God shall supply all your needs according to his riches in glory by Christ Jesus (Philippians 4:19).

It is God's Church, His ministry, and His gifts. If God cannot sustain the ministry through righteousness, who can?

Many believe that God tolerates and does not condemn sin because of His love for us. They forget that His patience and love should bring us to repentance and not lead us to accept an unholy life-style that is contrary to His Word.

> The Lord is not slack concerning his promise, as some men count slackness; but is longsuffering to us-ward, not willing that any should perish, but that all should come to repentence (2 Peter 3:9).

They destroy the faith of many who come to them seeking truth. Instead of correcting sinners, they condone their behavior, making them even worse.

> Woe unto you, scribes and Pharisees, hypocrites! for ye compass sea and land to make one proselyte, and when he is made, ye make him twofold more the child of hell than yourselves (Matthew 23:15).

A main attraction to Spirit-filled churches are the miracles and wonders of God being performed. Many will leave their church to attend a crusade or revival if they hear a prophet or healer is in town. Without a doubt miracles are still being performed in the Church today. Charlatans who do not flow in the power of God, however, have crept in unnoticed.

Turn on the television and you will see psychics claiming to reveal the future by tarot cards, palm reading, and other means all in the name of God. Not only are the television audiences deceived but so are many church members. They may not play with tarot cards, but they read their horoscopes. Some are still sending away for dust and potions to drive away evil spirits.

A sorcerer named Simon attached himself to the early church.

> But there was a certain man, called Simon, which beforetime in the same city used sorcery, and bewitched the people of Samaria, giving out that himself was some great one: To whom they all gave heed, from the least to the greatest, saying, This man is the great power of God. And to him they had regard, because that of long time he had bewitched them with sorceries (Acts 8:9-11).

We get the word *simony* from this sorcerer who tried to purchase the gifts of God from the apostles (Acts 8:19-24). Simony means the purchase and sale of ecclesiastical powers. Whenever the prophet will only come to your church or town for a specified amount of money, he is selling his gift and therefore performing a form of witchcraft.

Jesus said:

> Freely ye have received, freely give (Matthew 10:8).

In other words, the gifts of God were never meant to be hired out to the highest bidder. Instead the gifts of God are given freely that the Body of Christ may be perfected (Ephesians 4:11-13).

All gifts find their origin in the Holy Ghost, who directs you to Jesus Christ.

> Howbeit when he, the Spirit of truth, is come, he will guide you into all truth: for he shall not speak of himself; but whatsoever he shall hear, that shall he speak: and he will shew you things to come. He shall glorify me: for he shall receive of mine, and shall shew it unto you (John 16:13,14).

If someone is glorifying in what they can do and how wonderful they are, this is a form of witchcraft. God shares His glory with no one. Herod was smitten by the angel of the Lord because he did not give God the glory (Acts 12:20-23).

The apostle Paul predicted a departure from the faith precipitated by power and signs and lying wonders of Satan.

> And for this cause God shall send them strong delusion, that they should believe a lie (2 Thessalonians 2:11).

We cannot and must not be deceived by every supernatural event, believing it is from God.

The magicians in Pharaoh's court duplicated almost all the miracles that God performed at the hands of Moses. The devil has power, but he is powerless against a child of God because we have the Spirit of Christ living inside us. That's why the devil seeks to deceive us. He knows that he cannot overpower us because Jesus Christ fights our battles for us. If we are deceived, however, we provide an opening for the devil to come in. We can protect ourselves if we simply obey God's Word.

Jesus told His disciples:

Wherefore by their fruits ye shall know them (Matthew 7:20).

If people live a life of immorality, do not acknowledge Jesus as Lord and Savior, and are seeking filthy lucre, you can believe they are not of God. Do not follow them! If they don't give glory to the Father through Jesus Christ His Son, that's a good indication it's witchcraft.

Chapter Nine

The Religious Right–Is It Right?

A tidal wave of conservatism is sweeping the country called the Religious Right. And with it comes the traditions and values of a society many thought dead. This new wave of conservatism is opposed to legalized abortion, believes in creationism instead of evolution, believes homosexuality is a deviant and sinful life-style, and steadfastly believes in the traditional, autonomous family.

This wave of conservatism has as its underpinning the Bible, the Constitution of the United States of America, and the Declaration of Independence. These documents have proven to instill moral behavior, turned a fledgling collection of states into a great country, and granted civil liberties to those under its guidance. The success of our nation has served as a model for the rest of the world.

Why does the Religious Right place such credibility in these documents? They believe the United States was providentially founded by our forefathers who created the Declaration of Independence and Constitution in a Christian culture. This being the case, all thoughts and opinions in their interpretation are designed to direct a nation toward Christ. Secular humanism and liberal politicians have conspired to undermine the integrity of these documents. These groups and their sympathizers are seen as a threat not only to Christian culture in America but also the traditional moral values that made this nation great.

The Religious Right uses politics as its pulpit to deliver its message. Political decisions inflicted the most damage to their traditional causes. If they can control the political arena, or at least influence the political process, they can mitigate or altogether negate laws and decisions opposed to the conservative agenda. The harsher the laws passed by our legislature and decisions rendered by our Supreme Court, the more active they become.

Cultural Decay

The 1960s and 1970s were a time of great moral decline. This period caught conservative Christians unprepared as activists and organizers. Because there was no watchman on the wall, privileges Christians had taken for granted were being dismantled or outlawed as a new cultural climate set in. There was no Religious Right to serve as vigilante over matters of morals and righteousness. This led to the current cultural climate that seeks to downplay the importance of God and morality.

Situation ethics became the rule of the day. If it feels good, do it. Such attitudes have pitted liberals against the Religious Right. They believe they are in spiritual warfare for the soul of the country. Their loss would betray the cause of Jesus Christ and plunge the nation into further degeneracy.

Consider the impact of the 1963 Supreme Court decision *Abingdon vs. Schempp*, which took God out of the schools.

Lacking a moral compass, our public schools have become a police state. Metal detectors check for guns and knives. Teachers fear physical abuse at the hands of their students. Hostile climates in the classroom have created a vacuum devoid of learning. The decline in the public school system has motivated many to get politically involved. Within one generation they have seen what the removal of God from the public setting can do.

Defense and Fiscal Policy

Conservative Christian activism has bled over into other areas. Not only are they concerned about the moral climate but other interests affecting the country as well. Communism, which preaches the state is the ultimate authority, was enemy number one. It is considered an oxymoron to say that you are a communist and believe in God.

Because communism–before the collapse of the Soviet Union–was a threat to the United States, it was an enemy that had to be subjugated by armed force. President Ronald Reagan referred to the Soviet Union as "the evil empire." Being the poster boy for the Religious Right, Reagan inspired them to put pressure on their legislators to support increased defense spending. The Religious Right took the position that our survival as a nation was based on a strong defense. Not only did the Religious Right veer away from moral policy into such things as national defense, it also tapped into fiscal policy.

John Calvin was the progenitor of the Protestant Work Ethic. His doctrine of predestination taught that God had chosen those who would be saved from the foundation of the world. Since salvation was out of our hands, we would show forth the righteousness of God by our dedication to work.

The Protestant Work Ethic had a two-fold purpose. Not only did it teach that God wants us to be good stewards of our time here on earth by working it also benefited the industrial revolution, which was in its infancy. The agrarian population hesitated leaving the farm where they had security and the ability to provide for the family. The owners of factories during the industrial revolution had the technology but not the people to make them productive. The influence of John Calvin's predestination, with it's emphasis on work, directly addressed the shortfall in manpower the factories initially experienced.

The Protestant Work Ethic is dominant within the Religious Right because the majority of it's members are Protestants. Their bent toward work affects their perception of social programs. Deeply embedded within the Religious Right is the belief that everyone should work, which calls for the diminishing or scrapping of the welfare system created under the New Deal and the Great Society administrations.

Since the Religious Right has such an astounding, principled belief system, why do so many groups feel alienated by or outright oppose this new conservatism? To understand the opposition, let's look at some of the documents on which their belief system is based.

Who is Nature's God?

The Declaration of Independence the United States accepted on July 4, 1776 is a document many say was written in a Christian culture. In a country that cries out for separation of Church and state, we see in the founding document the mention of God and references to Him as creator. "When in the course of human events... Laws of Nature and of *Nature's God*.... that all men are *created equal*, that they are endowed by *their creator* with certain inalienable Rights, that among these are Life, Liberty, and the pursuit of Happiness."

Just who is this "Nature's God"? Greek mythology worships the deity Diana, the fertility goddess of the Ephesians. She was also called Mother Earth, which is a euphemism for nature. Is it a coincidence the Masons include the worship of nature in their formulas for advancement? The mention of Nature's God in the Declaration of Independence by the founding fathers shows that some purport to have been Masons.

In many schools today, recitation of the Declaration of Independence can be forbidden because of the reference to God. The 1963 Supreme Court decision precipitated the debate over how much can be said about God and by whom it can be said. The Supreme Court, before the 1963 decision, had taken the position that as long as it did not prefer one religion over another it was acceptable to let any religion espouse its beliefs.

Atheist Madelyn Murray O'Hare, one of the plaintiffs in the decision to remove religion from the school, objected to any mention of God by all religions. So the Christian Right takes the position that the Supreme Court went too far in excluding religion from school. How could the judicial system deny our schools the right to acknowledge God when our founding documents do?

If we look closely at the Declaration of Independence, we will notice something missing. Nowhere in the document is the name of Jesus Christ mentioned. Before Jesus Christ was manifested in the flesh, all religions of the world had a belief in a god. When Jesus Christ came on the scene, the New Testament states:

There is none other name under heaven given among men, whereby we must be saved (Acts 4:12).

That name is Jesus.

Whosoever therefore shall be ashamed of me and of my words in this adulterous and sinful generation; of him also shall the Son of man be ashamed, when he cometh in the glory of his Father with the holy angels (Mark 8:38).

The apostle Paul cried out:

I am not ashamed of the gospel of Christ: for it is the power of God unto salvation to every one that believeth (Romans 1:16).

Can you imagine the impact the founding document would have had if instead it said that Jesus Christ created us?

Giving thanks unto the Father... Who hath delivered us from the power of darkness, and hath translated us into the kingdom of his dear Son... For by him were all things created, that are in heaven, and that are in earth, visible and invisible, whether they be thrones, or dominions, or principalities, or powers: all things were created by him, and for him (Colossians 1:12,13,16).

If the authors were writing in a Christian culture, why were they not more expressive in pronouncing Jesus as Lord? The generic form of God used here leads to a wide view of interpretation. The Ten Commandments given to Moses as a guide for the nation of Israel is unequivocal in its pronunciation as to Who the author of the Commandments is and how Israel was to acknowledge Him (Exodus 34:27,28).

What About the Founding Fathers?

Our founding fathers may have been deists or Masons. Deists believe God created the earth and then stepped back from it. A God Who does not intercede in the affairs of men does not give revelation to men. In other words, deists believe men are self-sufficient and do not need God to mettle in their daily affairs.

The Bible says we are to call on the Lord daily:

Lord, I have called daily upon thee, I have stretched out my hands unto thee (Psalm 88:9).

Therefore, if they were deists, their understanding of Scripture was wrong.

Masonry, which I believe had a strong influence on the written founding documents, has a doctrine that the name of Jesus Christ is not to be invoked during their meetings. A Christian joining the order may choose whether or not he wants to believe that Jesus Christ is Lord and Savior. This is not a position taught by the Masons. Nowhere in Mason literature is Jesus referred to as God or portrayed as Savior. Instead they teach many gods lead to heaven. Masonry holds that Jesus was just a man. Scripture declares Masons are in error in what they teach and what they allow.

And without controversy great is the mystery of godliness: God was manifest in the flesh, justified in the Spirit, seen of angels, preached unto the Gentiles, believed on in the world, received up into glory (1 Timothy 3:16).

In other words, there is no debate. Scripture is forthright in proclaiming Jesus as God being manifest in the flesh. Therefore any group that does not acknowledge Jesus as Lord and Savior, such as the Masons, is heretical and should be rejected.

Who Do Masons Worship?

Many upstanding citizens belong to the Masons. They perform good deeds and support benevolent causes. We need to look beyond these external issues, however, to the heart of their beliefs. Just who do Masons worship?

Coil's Masonic Encyclopedia confesses:

There is no dispute between Freemasons and their fiercest critics that both the word Jehovah and the composite word, Jahbulon, appear on the [Masonic] altar, on top of which is inscribed a circle, containing a triangle. Around the circle is inscribed the name JEHOVAH and on the three sides of the triangle the letters JAH BUL ON....

To all of this must be added the third and final feature of the top of the pedestal: the Hebrew characters set at the angles of the triangle: Alif, Beth, and Lamed, each of which is said to have reference to the deity or to some divine attribute. Take each combination with the whole, and it will read thus: "Ab Bal, Father, Lord: Al Bal, Word, Lord; Lab Bal, Spirit, Lord."

Coil's Masonic Encyclopedia shows how deceptive the Masons are in doctrine. Masonry combines Baalism with the worship of Jehovah. Baal was a pagan god of the heathen nations whose worship included sexual perversion. The women paid their vows to the temple of Baal by prostitution. In other temples, sodomites (homosexuals) served the same purpose as the woman prostitutes. Jehovah vehemently spoke against such practices in the following verses:

There shall be no whore of the daughters of Israel, nor a sodomite of the sons of Israel. Thou shall not bring the hire of whore, or the price of a dog, into the house of the Lord thy God for any vow: for even both these are abomination unto the Lord thy God (Deuteronomy 23:17,18).

The nation of Israel confronted this despicable form of worship practiced by the followers of Baal, and God judged it as being sinful. Masons consider the use of Baal as benign whereby God says it totally opposes Who He is.

And Elijah came unto all the people, and said, How long halt ye between two opinions? if the Lord be God, follow him: but if Baal, then follow him. And the people answered him not a word (1 Kings 18:21).

Masons, do you understand what Elijah says to you? You cannot serve God and Baal too. But this is what they have attempted to do with the name Jahbulon.

We have access to Jehovah God through His Son Jesus Christ.

Jesus saith unto him, I am the way, the truth, and the life: no man cometh unto the Father, but by me (John 14:6).

The name of Jesus and worshipping Him separates the Christian faith from the other religions in the world. Without Jesus Christ and His Sonship or divinity, we have no Christian faith.

The Masonic Agenda

George Washington, the first President of the United States, was a Mason. He warmly supported a plan for having the states convene a convention for the purpose of writing the Constitution. This sheds further light on why the Constitution is not more dogmatic in its proclamation of Who the Creator is.

Masonic influence by George Washington and others, I believe, caused generic terms to be used for God because they did not want to omit their false god–Baal. This is why Masonry must be rejected at all costs. Masons have as their agenda a humanist society where everybody's god is god, which means nobody's god is God.

Masons are in positions of authority worldwide. If they can continue to put key people in position of leadership, they can bring about the one world rule that is spoken of in these apocalyptic verses:

113

And there was given unto him a mouth speaking great things and blasphemies; and power was given unto him to continue forty and two months. And he opened his mouth in blasphemy against God, to blaspheme his name, and his tabernacle, and them that dwell in heaven. And it was given unto him to make war with the saints, and to overcome them: and power was given him over all kindreds, and tongues, and nations (Revelation 13:5-7).

The apostle Paul shows that any worship not devoted to the true and living God is worship devoted to the devil.

What say I then? that the idol is anything, or that which is offered in sacrifice to idols is any thing? But I say, that the things which the Gentiles sacrifice, they sacrifice to devils, and not to God: and I would not that ye should have fellowship with devils (1 Corinthians 10:19,20).

Masons do not worship the Father through His Son Jesus Christ. Therefore, whether they know it or not, they are worshipping devils. The devil gives the beast his power to make war with the saints (Revelation 13:4-7). As Eve was duped by the serpent with enticing words, Masons are being duped with their idea of a grand utopia here on earth governed by man.

There's only one way to accomplish the goal of world domination: placing key people in key positions. They need positions of influence filled by Masons to carry out their agenda. Throughout the history of this nation, Masonic influence has continued. Unless we wise up to the deceptions of Satan, we will never be the true Christian nation many believe we can be.

Masonic author H. L. Haywood, in his book, *The Great Teachings of Masonry*, sets forth this group's objectives. "It is a world law, destined to change the earth into conformity with itself, and as a world power it is something superb, awe inspiring, godlike." *Mackey's Revised Encyclopedia of Freemasonry* illustrates this goal when it discloses that the mission of Masonry is "to banish from the world every source of enmity and hostility," "to destroy the pride of conquest and the pomp of war," and "to extend to nations the principles of Masonry." Over and over again world domination comes up.

Paul A. Fisher, who wrote a book called *Behind the Lodge Door*, observed that the Masons dominated the U.S. Supreme Court from 1941-1971. This may explain the decisions that shifted our nation away from a God-fearing society to a more secular society in this century.

The apostle Paul warned us about "spiritual wickedness in high places." We see it being played out before our very eyes with the Supreme Court decisions in this century.

> For we wrestle not against flesh and blood, but against principalities, against powers, against the rulers of the darkness of this world, against spiritual wickedness in high places (Ephesians 6:12).

I believe the Declaration of Independence had Masonic influence and therefore mitigated the influence God intended for this country through strong Christian leadership. Leaders and lay members alike within our churches must be admonished so that this heresy does not spread further and we can truly be a God-fearing nation.

Can We Trust Conservatives?

The Religious Right has attached itself, for the most part, to the Republican party, believing their positions are more in line with Judeo-Christian principles. The Republican party leadership, however, is involved with Masonry. Former Senate Majority leader and presidential candidate Bob Dole is a

33rd degree Mason. Senator Jesse Helms, with whom most conservatives strongly identify, is also a Mason. Anyone who has reached the level that Bob Dole has within Masonry should not be ignorant of the intent of the Masons. If these leaders are truly Christians, they should take the challenge of Elijah and reject the god of Baal and Masonry.

Masons are very subtle in their approach to new members. They believe in practicing good works, such as supporting the Shrine Hospital. In addition, you must swear that you believe in a Supreme Being before you can become a Mason. They make the Supreme Being sound like the true God revealed in the Bible. Because many people are ignorant of what the Bible says about Who God is, they are easily deceived. The trick is which Supreme Being do you believe in? Is it Jahbulon or Jehovah God as revealed in His Son Jesus Christ? Masonry is an abomination to God, but the Religious Right continues to cling to leaders who are a part of this abomination.

Today there is an ecumenical movement trying to bring the religions of the world together. George Bush, during his presidency, attended one of these gatherings in South America. At this environmental conference, convened for the purpose of preserving the earth, cults, Buddhists, Hindus, Catholics, Protestants, and Muslims gathered. They all spoke of their devotion to their god or gods and their theology.

I do not care how morally good a person may be, or ascetic, or learned, or gifted. He may hold traditional, conservative views. He may even be a Republican. If he does not receive Jesus Christ as the Son of God, however, he is lost.

For what fellowship hath righteousness with unrighteousness? and what communion hath light with darkness? (2 Corinthians 6:14).

If we love Jesus, we should not be ashamed of Him.

More Problems

There are other statements in the Declaration of Independence that contradict it being a Judeo-Christian document. "That to secure these rights, Governments are instituted among men, deriving their just powers from the consent of the governed." This sounds like something from the Humanist Manifesto. It attributes to men powers that only God can give, whether we acknowledge it or not. What does Scripture say?

> Let every soul be subject unto the higher powers. For there is no power but of God: the powers that be are ordained of God (Romans 13:1).

These powers to become a nation are given by God. All powers or authority to rule are given by God. You would think erudite men would have known that power of government comes from God and not from men. This document is exclusive. All documents that God gives to us are inclusionary because of His desire to see all souls saved.

A disparaging remark is made concerning the "merciless Indian Savages." This blanket statement smacks of prejudice. It makes the assumption as a document that all Indians are merciless and savages. Does this sound like a Christian document?

The Constitution of the United States has very serious misgivings as a Judeo-Christian document. The clause that has generated the most controversy among the Religious Right is the first amendment. "Congress shall make no law respecting an establishment of religion, or prohibiting the free exercise thereof; or abridging the freedom of speech, or of the press; or the right of the people peaceably to assemble, and to petition the Government for a redress of grievance."

This clause guaranteed that the nation will not prefer one religion over the other. When the Constitution was written, the cloud of state religion as practiced by England was still over the head of this new nation. Because the Church of England had been so dogmatic and unrelenting in its pronouncements, many felt the need to break away from the Church. America was seen as the land of opportunity for practicing your faith without interference from the Church. These religious freedoms were so precious to the founding fathers they wanted to be sure their right to worship would not be abridged again.

An Imperfect Document

The addition of the first ten amendments, which is called the Bill of Rights, shows the imperfection of the document. The First Amendment shows the document is not a Christian document. The establishment clause, as in the Declaration of Independence, compromises itself when it comes to proclaiming Who God is. This clause gave legitimacy to every religion in the world.

If they knew the truth about Jesus Christ, why not prefer it over all the false religions in the world? Either they did not know Jesus on a personal basis, or they did know but were not convicted enough to put a stronger statement in the Bill of Rights. This clause led to restriction in school prayer and the removal of anything concerning Jesus Christ. Christianity is considered just another religion. How could any born again believer let something like this happen if he truly knows Jesus Christ in a personal way? It is my contention that the writers of the Constitution did not know God in a personal way.

The majority of African Americans are conservative. Why does the Religious Right have a membership of only five percent African American? When blacks hear that the Declaration of Independence and the Constitution are documents to return to traditional family values, warnings signs automatically go off.

Thomas Jefferson, one of the principal drafters of the Declaration of Independence, owned slaves. Not only did he own slaves, but his document supported other slave owners for nearly 100 years. When black people hear traditional values, they see a return to slavery and separate but equal laws. Whites must communicate to blacks this is not the case.

Blacks remember America's racist past. The 13th amendment didn't abolish slavery until December 18, 1865. Even after the abolishment of slavery, this new freedom for the Negro had to be assured and his rights had to be guaranteed.

The 14th amendment gave civil rights protection to all citizens of the U.S. This happened because many southern states passed laws that restricted the rights of African Americans. The 15th amendment gave the African American the right to vote in 1869. These amendments passed much to the consternation of Southerners.

Many of you may say this shows how good the Constitution is for allowing such drastic changes. Yet, there are two other amendments that show the imperfection of this document. The 18th amendment prohibited the manufacture, sale, or transportation of intoxicating liquors on January 29, 1919. The 21st amendment repealed the 18th amendment on December 5, 1933.

This document is not immutable as God's law is. Because these founding documents are changeable, many African Americans are uneasy when they hear talk of returning to the "good old days," which represent slavery, restricted civil rights, and no voting rights.

As Christians we have a written text to guide us in making decisions. The Bible, the Word of God, is not exclusive or changeable. It has stood the test of time. Other documents—such as the Declaration of Independence, the Constitution, and all the amendments—are trivial and insignificant compared to God's Word.

The Religious Right must acknowledge that the Bible is the only sacred Book and not the founding documents.

Chapter Ten

Abstinence Is Not Deliverance

An attractive, single young woman told a minister about some of the problems she suffered since giving her life to Christ. First, because her small hometown did not offer many job opportunities, she had to leave her loving Christian parents to find work in a distant city. She couldn't find a church like the one back home. Finally, she struggled with the ever recurring theme among young people today. She had not found a husband with whom she could settle down.

Upon hearing the desperation in her voice, the minister asked how she handled her sexual desires. He wanted to know if her desire to marry was based solely on her desire to be sexually intimate.

"I've abstained from sexual intercourse for a long time, but I'm not a nun," she admitted. "If the right man came along, I would probably be sexually intimate with him even though we were not married."

Her attitude is widespread among many young people today. Because she had abstained from sexual intercourse for a period of time, she believed this justified her salvation. Most people decide to serve the Lord because of a religious experience or some form of conviction. Based on these experiences and convictions, they live an exemplary life for a while.

Do these experiences and convictions in and of themselves constitute salvation when the person reverts to the old habits from which he or she was supposedly delivered?

Salvation and Deliverance

If we want to be saved, we must understand deliverance. In the Bible the one word is translated two ways. The word "save" is *sozo* in Greek and *natssal* in Hebrew. Sometimes the word is used as deliver:

Thou shalt beat him with the rod, and shalt deliver his soul from hell (Proverbs 23:14).

At other times the word is used as saved:

The king saved us out of the hand of our enemies, and he delivered us out of the hand of the Philistines (2 Samuel 19:9).

In other words, there is no deliverance without salvation and no salvation without deliverance.

Deliverance means to rescue or provide safety from something or someone. If we say that we are saved, that means we have been delivered from something. If we return to that thing, however, can we truly say that we are delivered or saved?

The apostle Paul wrote:

But now, after that ye have known God, or rather are known

of God, how turn ye again to the weak and beggarly elements, whereunto ye desire again to be in bondage?" (Galatians 4:9).

Does our ability to suppress sinful desires for a season constitute salvation, or is there much more to it?

The apostle Paul asked:

Know ye not, that to whom ye yield yourselves servants to obey, his servants ye are to whom ye obey; whether of sin unto death, or of obedience unto righteousness? (Romans 6:16).

Your deliverance has not been accomplished if sin continues to reign in your mortal body.

Why do we need deliverance? Satan is the ruler of this world. We are held captive by him if we have not accepted Jesus as Lord and Savior (Galatians 4:3-5). This is the reason people cannot quit sinning. No matter how many counselors they have seen, or prescription drugs they take, true deliverance only comes through Jesus Christ.

Everything else is only a lie masquerading as the truth. No lie endures forever; it will be found out. Often a great conflict occurs between lies and the truth, however. We cannot successfully fight spiritual warfare without Jesus Christ.

For this purpose the Son of God was manifested, that he might destroy the works of the devil (1 John 3:8).

If we have not received Christ Jesus as Lord and Savior, we need deliverance. If we cannot resist the temptations of the world, we need deliverance. If God's Word is not the guide for our lives, we need deliverance.

The nation of Israel was chosen by God. Even though they were in captivity in Egypt, their relationship to God as His chosen people did not change. Even though Israel performed their rituals and maintained their religion through worship, they were not free. They had the relationship but they were still in bondage.

How many of us have confessed faith in Jesus Christ but found it difficult to refrain from sin? We loved God, but somehow it seems that our weakness to sin outweighs our love for God. Does this mean we are not saved? If an old habit creeps up on us again, have we lost our salvation?

To answer this question, we must understand that salvation is a process. If we do not understand the process, the consequences can be dire. Imagine baking a cake. If you put the eggs, butter, flour, and sugar into a hot oven without first mixing the ingredients, you will not have a cake. The ingredients for a properly mixed cake and one that has not been mixed are the same. One has gone through the process of preparation the other has not. Our salvation is very similar.

Spirit, Soul, and Body

The process of salvation involves bringing the three parts of our being into agreement with each other. Before they can be brought into agreement, we must understand the role of each part.

We are tripartite beings composed of spirit, soul, and body.

And the very God of peace sanctify you wholly; and I pray God your whole spirit and soul and body be preserved blameless unto the coming of our Lord Jesus Christ (1 Thessalonians 5:23).

Each part of our total self has a part to play in our salvation. The spirit is the part from God that gives life. It is the spirit that quickeneth [gives life]; the flesh profiteth nothing (John 6:63).

Without the spirit there is no life to the body. The spirit does not contain your emotions and thoughts, but the soul does.

But now we are delivered from the law, that being dead wherein we were held; that we should serve in newness of spirit (Romans 7:6).

Our spirit enables us to respond to God.

When Adam disobeyed God in the Garden of Eden, he suffered physical and spiritual death. God told Adam, "For in the day that thou eatest thereof thou shalt surely die" (Genesis 2:17). Eve, who had not received direct instruction from God, was subsequently seduced by the cunning words of the serpent and ate the fruit.

Not only was Eve seduced, but she also seduced Adam to eat the fruit. Based on his disobedience, death took place. Adam and Eve did not drop dead physically that day, however. After their disobedience God banished them from the Garden of Eden. They went on to have children, and Adam lived to a very old age.

Did God lie? No! Death did take place in the Garden of Eden, but it was spiritual not physical. Spiritual death is separation from God. This is why Jesus told Nicodemus:

Verily, I say unto thee, Except a man be born of water and of the Spirit, he cannot enter into the kingdom of God.... Marvel not that I said unto thee, Ye must be born again (John 3:5,7).

When Adam sinned in the Garden, he became separated from God. How could this relationship be restored? That spiritual connection had to be reestablished. When a person receives Jesus Christ as Lord and Savior, the Father accepts His perfect sacrifice as a substitute for our death (1 John 2:2). This acceptance reestablishes our relationship with God.

Because of sin, the body also dies. We know that Adam did not live forever. After the Fall, God pronounced a curse upon the first couple, beginning with the man.

> In the sweat of thy face shalt thou eat bread, till thou return unto the ground; for out of it wast thou taken: for dust thou art, and unto dust shalt thou return (Genesis 3:19).

The body's origin is earthly while the Spirit's origin is heavenly. Upon death there is a return to the source from which the part of the tripartite being originated. The apostle Paul addressed this issue:

> Now this I say, brethren, that flesh and blood cannot inherit the kingdom of God (1 Cor. 15:50).

This curse has endured upon mankind from Adam even until now. While we are enduring the curse, the flesh strives to please itself. It does not know anything about heaven and has no desire to go to heaven.

The Battleground

The third part of the tripartite being is where the battle really takes place—the soul. God breathed the breath of life into the man created from the dust of the earth, and Adam "became a living soul" (Genesis 2:7). The flesh houses the soul and spirit. When a person is not born again, his spirit has no active influence over the soul. How can the spirit affect the soul? The curse of Adam must be negated by the born again experience. You cannot do the things of God if you have not been born again. A person is left to manipulation by the world and Satan.

The spirit's desire is to be with God. The flesh wants to indulge in the pleasures of the world. Your soul is in the middle, feeling the strong tug of spirit and flesh. When you are saved, your spirit is made alive in Jesus Christ. Your spirit rejoices in contacting the Father. When a person dies, their spirit returns to God.

Then shall the dust return to the earth as it was: and the spirit shall return unto God who gave it (Ecclesiastes 12:7).

Your flesh has no desire to be saved, however. It was made from the earth, and that's where it will return. Your flesh and spirit become enemies of each other. A great battle ensues for your soul.

You must first accept Jesus Christ as Lord and Savior to enable your spirit to respond to God the Father. Then you must bring the flesh under subjection. This is the tough part. That's why the spirit is first regenerated.

Walk in the Spirit, and ye shall not fulfil the lust of the flesh (Galatians 5:16).

The spirit of man communicates with the Spirit of God. This communication directs the believer in living a godly life. The Spirit of God shows us how to bring the flesh under subjection. When we are spirit controlled instead of flesh controlled, we have total deliverance. That is why the apostle Paul wrote that their "whole spirit and soul and body be preserved blameless unto the coming of our Lord Jesus Christ" (1 Thessalonians 5:23).

It's a Heart Issue

Unfortunately, Christians often judge according to the flesh. Is a babe in Christ saved if he or she is not demonstrating a mature Christian walk? It depends on the condition of the heart.

But God be thanked, that ye were the servants of sin, but ye have obeyed from the *heart* that form of doctrine which was delivered you (Romans 6:17).

The word obeyed means to submit without reservation.

If a person purposes in his heart to serve God but falters along the way because he has not mastered the flesh, he is not lost. It is not the outward manifestation but the inward decision of the heart that determines the destination of man.

Unfortunately, many deny the truth and set themselves up for strong delusion.

And for this cause God shall send them strong delusion, that they should believe a lie; that they all might be damned who believed not the truth, but had pleasure in unrighteousness (2 Thessalonians 2:11,12).

In other words, God desires our heart.

Out of the abundance of the heart the mouth speaketh (Matthew 12:34).

What is in the heart determines who the man is.

A young lady was raped by her brother at the age of nine. When her parents found out, they severely punished the boy. This girl continued on with her life with no guilt or hatred toward her brother.

Later in adult life, however, the pundits stirred guilt in her and hatred toward her brother. This guilt and hatred was only stilted when a counselor told her that an incident does not make a person. Because she had forgiven her brother from her heart, this determined who she is–not a woman who had been raped but a woman who had forgiven.

Just as the decision from her heart determined who she is, our decision from our heart determines who we are in Jesus Christ. God knows the flesh is weak, and He makes an allowance for it by providing grace. We must not deceive ourselves, however. If our heart is not right, it does not avail us of God's grace.

This is why the Church is in turmoil today. We do not see the effort within the heart of one seeking God. We may condemn these newborn Christians when they have not gone through the process of being a Christian.

Let us consider the saints in the New Testament. Peter denied the Lord. Mark deserted the work of God and the apostle Paul. Paul and Barnabas had such a bitter falling out that they had to separate. These were all great men of God, but they were not perfect. They were quick to acknowledge their shortcomings and make it right with God. They did not justify their shortcomings but confessed and repented from them.

Rather than admit that we have a shortcoming, however, we accept the sin in our life.

Worship God

How then does a person gain deliverance? The demoniac that Jesus met in the country of the Gadarenes gained his deliverance by worshipping Jesus.

And they came over unto the other side of the sea, into the country of the Gadarenes. And when he was come out of the ship, immediately there met him out of the tombs a man with an unclean spirit....

But when he saw Jesus afar off, he ran and worshipped him, and cried with a loud voice, and said, What have I to do with thee, Jesus, thou Son of the most high God? I adjure thee by God, that thou torment me not. For he said unto him, Come out of the man, thou unclean spirit....

And they come to Jesus, and see him that was possessed with the devil, and had the legion, sitting, and clothed, and in his right mind: and they were afraid (Mark 5:1,2,6-8,15).

To understand how the demoniac gained his deliverance, we must know what worship involves.

Jesus addressed the problem of worship:

But the hour cometh, and now is, when the *true worshippers* shall worship the Father in spirit and in truth: for the Father seeketh such to worship him (John 4:23).

Worship means to submit or make oneself low. This can be seen by the position taken by worshipers in biblical times. They prostrated themselves to show their humbleness or lowly position in relationship to God.

After we have humbled ourselves before God, we commune with God by the spirit. This can only happen, however, if we have been born again. Then to maintain that connection, we must dwell in the truth as revealed in God's Word.

Obey the Words of Jesus

Worship is just the beginning of deliverance. We must also obey the words of Jesus. Because a man heeded the words of the Son of God, his lunatic son was delivered.

Lord, have mercy on my son: for he is lunatick, and sore vexed: for ofttimes he falleth into the fire, and oft into the water. And I brought him to thy disciples, and they could not cure him.

Then Jesus answered and said, O faithless and perverse generation, how long shall I be with you? how long shall I suffer you? bring him hither to me. And Jesus rebuked the devil; and he departed out of him: and the child was cured from that very hour (Matthew 17:15-18).

Jesus asked, "Why call ye me, Lord, Lord, and do not the things which I say?" (Luke 6:46). He also said, "If a man love me, he will keep my words: and my Father will love him, and we will come unto him, and make our abode with him" (John 14:23).

Your total deliverance is directly related to your obedience to God's Word. When you yield yourself to God's Word, the Father and Son come to live with you. If They are living with you, you'll have the strength you need to get and maintain your deliverance.

Sometimes our deliverance is gradual. In the same way that it takes an hour to bake a cake, so our deliverance may take time.

Jesus knows how to administer your healing:

Then was brought unto him one possessed with a devil, blind, and dumb: and he healed him, insomuch that the blind and dumb both spake and saw (Matthew 12:22).

The word healed is the word *therapeuo.*

We get our word therapy from this Greek word. In its original form, the word meant to serve in a menial way, such as attending to a family member during an illness. In other words, the healing is gradual and not instantaneous. Healing and deliverance are at times used interchangeably.

Who his own self bare our sins in his own body on the tree, that we, being dead to sins, should live unto righteousness: by whose stripes ye were healed (1 Peter 2:24).

The healing spoken of here is from sin. Do not give up on your salvation because you are not where you desire to be. Continue striving for righteousness. In seeking God, you purify your soul.

The most important thing is that you not return to the sin from which you were delivered.

> When the unclean spirit is gone out of a man, he walketh through dry places, seeking rest, and findeth none. Then he saith, I will return into my house from whence I came out; and when he is come, he findeth it empty, swept, and garnished. Then goeth he, and taketh with himself seven other spirits more wicked than himself, and they enter in and dwell there: and the last state of that man is worse than the first (Matthew 12:43-45).

Getting free is one thing; staying free is another. Many Christians lack the discipline to renew their minds, avoid enticing situations, and sever bad relationships that will only drag them down.

Don't be an empty vessel that attracts demonic influence. Read and meditate on Scripture and ask God to fill you with the Holy Spirit. God delights in filling us again and again. Yield your life to God, resist the enemy, and position yourself in the victory that Christ has won for you.

> Stand fast therefore in the liberty wherewith Christ hath made us free, and be not entangled again with the yoke of bondage (Galatians 5:1).

I trust this book has opened your eyes to various deceptions that have infiltrated our society and the Church. May you always seek the truth and walk in the glorious freedom that Jesus Christ has made available to everyone who believes in Him.

Help Me! I've Fallen

by T. D. Jakes

"Help! I've fallen, and I can't get up." This cry, made popular by a familiar television commercial, points out the problem faced by many Christians today. Have you ever stumbled and fallen with no hope of getting up? Have you been wounded and hurt by others? Are you so far down you think you'll never stand again? Don't despair. All Christians fall from time to time. Life knocks us off balance, making it hard – if not impossible – to get back on our feet. The cause of the fall is not as important as what we do while we're down. T. D. Jakes explains how – and Whom – to ask for help. In a struggle to regain your balance, this book is going to be your manual to recovery! Don't panic. This is just a test!

Becoming A Leader

by Myles Munroe

Many consider leadership to be no more than staying ahead of the pack, but that is a far cry from what leadership is. Leadership is deploying others to become as good as or better than you are. within each of us lies the potential to be an effective leader. *Becoming A Leader* uncovers the secrets of dynamic leadership that will show you how to be a leader in your family, school, community, church and job. No matter where you are or what you do in life this book can help you to inevitably become a leader. Remember: it is never too late to become a leader. As in every tree there is a forest, so in every follower there is a leader. ***Workbook also available***

The God Factor

by James Giles

Is something missing in your life? Do you find yourself at the mercy of your circumstances? Is your self-esteem at an all-time low? Are your dreams only a faded memory? You could be missing the one element that could make the difference between success and failure, poverty and prosperity, and creativity and apathy. Knowing God supplies the creative genius you need to reach your potential and realize your dream. You'll be challenged as James Giles shows you how to tap into your God-given genius, take steps toward reaching your goal, pray big and get answers, eat right and stay healthy, prosper economically and personally, and leave a lasting legacy for your children.

The Biblical Principles of Success
Arthur L. Mackey, Jr.

There are only three types of people in the world: People who make things happen, People who watch things happen, and People who do not know what in the world is happening. *The Biblical Principles of Success* will help you become one who makes things happen. Success is not a matter of "doing it my way." It is turning from a personal, selfish philosophy to God's outreaching, sharing way of life. This powerful book teaches you how to tap into success principles that are guaranteed – *the Biblical principles of success!*

The Flaming Sword
by Tai Ikomi

Scripture memorization and meditation bring tremendous spiritual power, however many Christians find it to be an uphill task. Committing Scriptures to memory will transform the mediocre Christian to a spiritual giant. This book will help you to become addicted to the powerful practice of Scripture memorization and help you obtain the victory that you desire in every area of your life. *Flaming Sword* is your pathway to spiritual growth and a more intimate relationship with God.

Come, Let Us Pray!
by J. Emmette Weir

Like an ocean, prayer is so vast that we will never plumb its depths. Are you content to walk along the shore, or are you ready to launch out into the deep? No matter what your stage of spiritual development, you can learn to pray with greater intimacy, gratitude, and power. Discover the secrets of personal prayer in *Come, Let Us Pray!*

Available at your local bookstore